The Tao of
Voice

THE TAO of
VOICE

A New East-West Approach to Transforming the Singing and Speaking Voice

STEPHEN CHUN-TAO CHENG 程俊濤

Foreword by JEAN HOUSTON

Destiny Books
Rochester, Vermont

Destiny Books
One Park Street
Rochester, Vermont 05767

LIBRARY OF CONGRESS CATALOGING-IN-PUBLICATION DATA

Cheng, Stephen Chun-Tao.
    The Tao of voice : a new East-West approach to transforming the singing and speaking voice / by Stephen Chun-Tao Cheng.
        p.   cm.
    Includes bibliographical references.
    1. Singing—Methods. 2. Taoism. I. Title.
    MT850.C52 1989
    783'.04—dc20   89-17187
                                            CIP
                                          MN

Printed and bound in the United States

10 9 8 7 6 5 4

Photographs by Ed Wissner.

Text art by Annamie Curlin and Virginia L. Scott.

Illustration on page 106 by Elaine Foster. Calligraphy by Annamie Curlin.

Destiny Books is a division of Inner Traditions International

Distributed to the book trade in Canada by Publishers Group West (PGW), Toronto, Ontario

Distributed to the book trade in the United Kingdom by Deep Books, London

Distributed to the book trade in Australia by Millennium Books, Newtown, N.S.W.

Distributed to the book trade in New Zealand by Tandem Press, Auckland

Distributed to the book trade in Europe by HDG Distrirep, The Netherlands

Distributed to the book trade in South Africa by Alternative Books, Randburg

CONTENTS

Acknowledgments

I wish to express my deep appreciation to Mia Grosjean, my agent, yet more than an agent, a true friend who worked with heart and soul alongside me on this book, and to Jean Houston, whose teaching has been a great source of inspiration.

I am grateful for the advice and help of editors Leslie Colket, Susan Davidson, and Susan Keniston, and art director Estella Arias. I also wish to acknowledge the creative effort of art designers Elaine Foster, Leslie Phillips, and Annamie Curlin.

I wish to thank Mavis Moore and Earl Price for their help in making this book possible, Alexandra Soteriou for introducing me to Mia Grosjean, and Da Liu for his counsel. Thank you also to stage directors Frank Corsaro and Joshua Logan for their guidance. The following teachers have been of great help to me: Alexander Kipnis, Hardesty Johnson, Harry R. Wilson, Emanuel Balaban, and Sergius Kagen.

I also express here my deep appreciation for those friends and students who over the years have encouraged my efforts in developing *The Tao of Voice,* in particular Dean Herbert London of New York University and Stella Adler, whose enlightening teaching has helped me gain a deeper insight into the art of acting.

I wish to express my gratitude to Chen Chi, who, in the Chinese tradition, is my esteemed "big brother," for letting me use a detail from one of his paintings for my book cover.

This book is dedicated to people who use their voices to promote peace and harmony around the world.

FOREWORD

There is an ancient story that comes out of old China about a peasant whose horse ran away. When his neighbors offered their sympathies because of his misfortune, he simply responded, "Maybe." The following day his horse returned bringing with it six wild horses. His neighbors returned, this time to express their surprise and pleasure at his good luck. Again he said, "Maybe." The next day his son, attempting to ride one of the wild horses, was thrown and broke his leg. The neighbors were sympathetic in this turn of his fortune, but again the farmer simply said, "Maybe." The next day saw the arrival of conscription officers, forcing the young men to join the army. The officers passed over the young man because of his broken leg. The neighbors gathered to exclaim how well it all had worked out, but again the farmer simply said, "Maybe."

The farmer, a classic Taoist type, sensed his life as part of a much larger pattern of unfolding, which had its own circularity and which allowed for the interplay of opposite forces. Time's rhythm was the vehicle of that unfolding, so one knew that there was no such thing as a final activity and therefore one could only suspend judgement and let the Tao flow where it may.

How different from Western approaches is the Chinese Taoist perspective of seeing the circular potency of all things, the One unified and flowing through the many. How different this is from the Newtonian notion of a universe set into motion by an original act of creation, and allowed to continue running on its own hardwired programs independent of the Creator. This ultimately makes of reality a series of mechanical happenings, working itself out in an infinitely complex latticework of separate causal sequences acting and interacting through history. We in the West who are still bearing the brunt of this outmoded mechanistic view suffer from chronic tunnel vision, training ourselves to look for cause and effect in all aspects of our world and work. This makes for strained artistic expression and separatist notions of our place in the reality. Thus we fail to see as the Taoists do the interacting patterns inherent in the causal weave of connections.

What we call Taoism reflects this causal weave, for it has so many myriad forms, so many facets, so much whimsy and high play, so profound a philosophical base, so wild and woolly a magical and alchemical past that virtually no one is able to define it with authority. It incorporates the wisdom and findings of millennia, from the occult and healing practices of the fabled Yellow Emperor of the third millennium B.C. to the philosophy expounded almost two and a half thousand years ago in the works of the sages Lao Tzu and Chuang Tzu, to the findings of yogins steeped in the arts of rejuvenation, prolonging life, and achieving one of the several kinds of immortality. To mystics seeking union with the Sublime Tao, it meant the cultivation of practices derived from both the philosophical and yogic treatises, so as to prepare body and mind for coherence and co-creativity with Nature and the One. Many Taoists are involved with the entire weave of these teachings and practices.

Taoist philosopher and singing teacher Stephen Chun-Tao Cheng is surely one of the finest living exponents of this complex natural philosophy and in *The Tao of Voice* offers an interpretation found in the *Tao Teh Ching* that when things are allowed to take their natural course they move with a wonderful perfection and harmony. This is because, in such case, the Tao (the eternal Way of the universe) is not hindered in its smooth operation. When applied to the development of the voice this becomes a unique method of evoking a depth and breadth of vocal expression that is at once as beautiful as it is enjoyable for the vocalist to express. The painful and plodding practices of Western vocal calisthenics and programs of effecting specific ends from specific vocal techniques are avoided in Cheng's brilliant artistic philosophy and practice. Here one finds an overall development, one that promotes physical as well as spiritual and emotional enhancement. One grows as one sings, and one sings the awakening of one's being.

Cheng offers the student ways of felicitously combining the great breathing exercises of Taoist practice with state-of-the-art methods of psychophysical reeducation for the voice and the entire body. Thus the Taoist principles of the continuous circular movement of breath through the body and the interplay of opposite forces are presented as integral to any profound psychophysical development. What occurs from this is mindfulness, the supreme practice of any art of body, mind, or spirit.

Cheng shows how to develop the kinesthetic as well as the imaginal sense of singing, how to enhance the body image in performance while toning the voice with emotional presence. Vocal expressions made in the kinesthetic imagination are shown to have positive results in actual singing. Throughout this book Cheng demonstrates exercises that provide for a simultaneous working with body, mind, and spirit to achieve the aimed-for results. Naturally there is also improvement in cognitive and feeling functions, for the extensive changes in the brain's motor cortex that must precede changes in the muscular system affect adjacent brain areas as well and have a salutary effect on thinking and feeling. Singing becomes a joy, an art and a mystery, a gift of healing of the self and others. Distortions in the body image are cured as a refined awareness is sought and found. In classical Taoist fashion such awareness is cultivated as a habit, becomes the singer's natural state, and is, for that reason, effortless.

It is a sad truism that many singers as well as others who employ their bodies for their art—dancers, muscians, athletes—can deform their physical instrument because their awareness is only partial. Thus they often damage themselves out of the need to surpass themselves, forcing their bodies into outrageous and damaging development in order to "win" and "achieve" a questionable goal.

Or, as the *Tao Teh Ching* so eloquently states:

Stretch a bow to the full,
And you will wish you had stopped in time;
Temper a sword-edge to its very sharpest,
And you will find it soon grows dull.

With the methods presented in *The Tao of Voice* such foolish practices can be done away with altogether, as the sacred conjunction of the findings of East and West brings a renewal of human possibility and a reenchantment of the world through high speech and holy song.

To know harmony is to know the Always-so.
To know the Always-so is to be awakened.

Dr. Jean Houston

INTRODUCTION

The Great Tao flows everywhere . . . . It nourishes the myriad things.

LAO TZU

Let your voice and being flow with the Tao.

THE AUTHOR

It is a joyful feeling to experience the transformation of one's voice, a one-of-a-kind instrument that expresses one's thoughts and emotions more directly than any other. In this book I wish to share with you my approach to this transformation process. While there are other methods, I offer my approach as an alternative to those of you who are seeking new ways to realize the full potential of your voice.

The Tao of Voice is based on courses I have taught in vocal technique and singing at the New School for Social Research, New York University, the Stella Adler Conservatory of Acting in New York City, and other institutions. The book springs from years of study as well as from my performances as a singer and actor in concert, television, film, and Broadway productions. The book is primarily designed to help its readers to improve their voices and to enhance the arts of singing and speaking through a method of conditioning derived from the harmonious union of Eastern and Western wisdom.

My approach unifies, for the first time, the best of Western vocal technique and ancient Chinese philosophy and breathing practices, as well as important psychophysical discoveries of my own. These discoveries are used throughout *The Tao of Voice* in many exercises, including body movement exercises and exercises for breathing and singing with continuous circular movement. These same principles also inform the chapters on technique and vocal exercises. Based on a harmonious fusion of feeling, visualization, and body movements, they are applied to channel users into a healthy altered state where they can let their voices flow through difficult vocal obstacles, thereby achieving their goals.

Through the years of using this Taoist approach, I have had marked results in helping myself and many others. With this approach, improvement of tonal quality and power and extension of vocal range and dynamics can be achieved within a reasonably short period of time. The Taoist approach also helps to develop the harmonious attitude, poise, and stage presence essential to a performing artist. This method can help singers and non-singers alike to develop vocal color and identity, practice effectively, cure voice breaks, overcome stage fright, facilitate expressive communication and performance, and maintain good mental and physical health—vital components of maintaining a healthy voice. This book will be of value whether or not the reader is studying voice formally. It will help to open up a new channel for the voice as well as for personal growth and transformation.

Though most of the material of this book is addressed to singers, those who do not sing but want to improve their speaking voices can benefit a great deal by absorbing the philosophy in the book and by practicing the specially designed exercises. Readers can begin with the exercises they feel comfortable with and then gradually pick up the others.

We all know that expressive and beautiful singing gives joy to the singer and to the listener. It elevates our spirit and opens up the channels of our being to receive blessings from the universe. There are times in life when we feel good because we have just sung a song that pleases us, even though we can't really sing the song well. Without a doubt, singing affects our lives in a positive way!

Through singing I have become more aware and appreciative of the warm and glowing quality of people and Nature and believe that developing this awareness can create a richer, warmer tonal quality. Such appreciation can bring people together, producing good feelings and lasting friendships. It inspires us to recognize that we are a part of Nature and that Nature is a part of ourselves. Consider this: The character for music in China is 樂 pronounced "yueh." The same character also means happy or happiness when it is pronounced "lo." This implies that music and happiness are very closely related; they can even become one. I earnestly hope that those of you who do not sing now will let this book help you learn to sing, and that those who do sing will keep singing, so that you will all let the joy of music and song enrich your life.

1

Philosophical Basis

Tao is great, active, far-reaching and cyclical in its movement.

LAO TZU

The Roots of Taoism

My approach to singing stems from the best of Western vocal technique and from the teachings of Taoism, a Chinese philosophy the roots of which have been traced back to the legendary sage Fu Shi, who lived about 3000 B.C.

The first important writings on Taoist philosophy were found much later in the *I Ching* and *The Book of Tao and Power*. The basis for the *I Ching* was the writing of King Wen, dated around 1143 B.C., and of his son, Tan, the Duke of Chou, who wrote around thirty years later. These works were presented by Confucius, with his commentaries, in the famous book the *I Ching,* nearly five hundred years later. Also known as *The Book of Changes,* it has become a very important Chinese classic, consulted as a common source for both Confucian and Taoist philosophies.

The Book of Tao and Power,[1] a philosophical commentary on the Tao, is attributed to the work of Lao Tzu in the sixth century B.C. Both this book and the *I Ching* formed the basis for further exploration of Taoist philosophy by other brilliant scholars, notably Chuang Tzu in the third century B.C. By the sixth century A.D., Taoism had become firmly established as one of the major religions and philosophies in China.

While surely an important Eastern theology, however, Taoism is not simply a system of quiet contemplation or idle speculation. It is also a practical philosophy and has had far-reaching influences in the arts, science, medicine, health, and other fields. (See the Bibliography at the end of this book for books on Taoism.) Tao, in its broadest sense, is the natural way of functioning in the universe. It is a path followed by natural events. It is characterized by spontaneous creativity, the dynamic and harmonious interplay of opposite forces or elements, and a regular and orderly sequence of natural phenomena such as spring following winter and night following day.

Taoism adds intuitive wisdom to rational knowledge. In his *Tao of Physics*, Fritjof Capra points out that the careful observation of Nature, combined with a strong mystical intuition, led the Taoist sages of old to profound insights that are confirmed today by scientific theories. Capra thinks that one of the most important insights of Taoism is the realization that transformation and change are essential features of Nature, manifested by the dynamic interplay of opposites.[2] Capra also relates this concept to a statement made by the Greek thinker Heraclitus, who lived in the sixth century B.C. and is often mentioned in connection with modern physics. In asserting that "everything flows," Heraclitus shared Lao Tzu's emphasis on continuous and cyclic change in Nature.[3]

The value of Tao lies in its power to reconcile opposites on a higher level of consciousness. "To reconcile the polarities in order to achieve a balanced way of living and a higher integration is the endeavor of psychotherapy," wrote the noted Taoist author Chang Chung-yuan in his book *Creativity and Taoism,* when he related Taoism to modern psychology.[4] The prominent psychiatrist Carl Jung revealed in 1929 that he had unconsciously used Taoist principles in treating his patients.[5]

Yin and Yang and the Supreme Ultimate

To understand the basis of my vocal technique, we must look into Taoism. We must try to understand the diagram of the Supreme Ultimate, shown in Figure 1, and the concepts that it holds.

FIGURE 1

The basis of Taoist philosophy states that opposites or polarities—yin and yang—exist in everything and everywhere. For instance, yin originally referred to the shady side of the mountain, and yang, the sunny side. Female is yin, male is yang; softness is yin, firmness is yang; yielding is yin, pushing is yang. Yin and yang are a pair of complementary forces that act in the universe unceasingly. To eliminate one is to destroy the other.

In singing, the opposites include loud and soft volume, high and low notes, fast and slow tempos, and inhaling and exhaling breath. This dynamic philosophy, which the Taoist calls the "interplay of opposite forces," can best be shown by the ancient Chinese symbol T'ai Chi Tu, or the diagram of the Supreme Ultimate. It was created in China about 1200 A.D. Before that, other symbols had been developed to signify the Supreme Ultimate, but this one in particular has lasted through the ages and remains the most widely used.

The diagram synthesizes two very important Taoist concepts, that of continuous circular movement and that of the interplay of opposite forces. Being able to visualize and understand these two concepts in motion is pertinent to my vocal technique. The diagram of the Supreme Ultimate shows the dark yin and the bright yang. It shows both the rotational and symmetrical relationship of yin and yang through the dynamic interplay of opposite forces. The two very small circles in the diagram symbolize the idea that within the yang there is yin, and within the yin there is yang. The balance between the two opposites symbolizes their essential interdependence.

The diagram has two fishlike figures that illustrate continuous circular movement within the circle. The curved dividing line symbolizes constant flowing energy from one force into the other, a give and take that is essential to continuous circular movement. This is the movement of Tao.

The importance of continuous circular movement and the interplay of opposite forces was pointed out and described by Lao Tzu:

> Tao is great, active, far-reaching and cyclical in its movement. . . .
> It is unchanging as oneness, unceasing, and ever-revolving.

Lao Tzu's words evoke wonderful imagery for the voice and for singing. The imagery imparted by a concept, a method, or a teacher to a singer has a great deal to do with positive or negative responses from the singer. These Taoist thoughts are the roots from which my approach has grown. Thus, what distinguishes it from others is mainly the application of these concepts of continuous circular movement and the interplay of opposite forces (yin and yang), along with the adaptation of deep breathing from T'ai Chi exercises and my own psychophysical technique.

Visualization is a very important part of the latter. When you visualize the concepts of the interplay of opposite forces and continuous circular movement at the same time, you might be imagining the movement of a gyroscope or even a top. This movement is both horizontal and vertical and flows in and out, creating the energy for maintaining balance. This, along with the feeling of flowing energy, is an essential part of the Tao of voice.

The Wonder of Continuous Circular Movement

In good singing there is only one voice—a smooth, seamless voice without breaks—although for convenience singers refer to different registers, such as head and chest, or head voice and chest voice. The balance of the voice in the head and the chest registers and the flow of the voice from one register into another are paramount in producing a free and good voice. Continuous circular movement can help achieve this balance.

In virtually any realm of life, continuous circular movement can do wonders. Oftentimes we can see it right around us. It can be found in the wheel and its many forms, including record players and records, video and computer discs, and cassette players. The breast stroke and the crawl in swimming, the discus throw, and even walking and running are all activities that use the wonder of circular movement. It is also in the motion of the gyroscope used in the scientific world.

During the early sixteenth century, Leonardo da Vinci used circles for calisthenics and dance movements. For him, it stood for the movement of the Earth on its axis.[6] In China today, continuous circular movement and the interplay of opposite forces are actively applied in the supreme national health exercise, T'ai Chi Ch'uan. Over the last decade, this form of exercise has also been gaining popularity in many parts of the world, especially in the United States. Its development is credited to Chang San-feng, a Taoist who lived around the thirteenth century. This exercise is believed to lead many practitioners to health, happiness, and long life, because it relaxes the body and mind, quiets the nervous system, benefits the heart and blood circulation, makes joints move better, and helps digestion. The coordination of the body, mind, and spirit stimulates the steady flow of the breath energy or vital energy (ch'i) and is essential in the practice of T'ai Chi Ch'uan. I believe this is also vital to good voice production.

Because circular movement and the dynamic interplay of opposite forces are used so extensively in T'ai Chi, I have selected two basic exercise forms and modified them for your use. Called the Golden Rooster and Moving Meditation (see Chapter 3), they are easy to learn; daily practice of these exercises will help you relax and center yourself, breathe deeply, generate unforced energy flow for singing or speaking, and, most importantly, be in tune with the Tao by creating a balance of your body, mind, and spirit.

Taoist meditation, which is a vital part of everyday life for many Chinese, also applies continuous circular movement. The Taoist lifestyle comes from careful study that combines meditation and daily physical health practices which have developed over the centuries. The meditation that uses continuous circular movement is called Meditation with Grand Circle. This can be done in various ways. In one method, the circle starts at a spot between and behind the eyebrows, which the Taoist calls the "center of spirit" (Tsu-Ch'iao).[7] Total concentration on this center is considered paramount to spiritual growth and advancement. The grand circle continues from there toward the "center of vital energy" (Tan-T'ien), which is located in the lower abdomen, about two inches below the navel. In this Taoist meditation practice, breath is imagined to flow from the center of spirit toward the center of vital energy and then back, in a continuous circular movement.

When meditating you should imagine, while inhaling, that your breath goes down from the center of spirit to the center of vital energy. While exhaling, imagine that your breath continues down from the center of vital energy, back toward the base of the spine, up the spinal column, passing through the back of the neck and up over the crown of the head, once again reaching the center of spirit. As you begin to inhale again you start all over.

This Meditation with Grand Circle can also be done in a reverse circular movement. You imagine, while inhaling from the center of spirit, that your breath goes up over the crown of the head, down the back of the neck and the spinal column to the base of the spine, then from the base of the spine to the center of vital energy. Then while exhaling, your breath flows upward from the center of vital energy, reaching the center of spirit once again. As you begin to inhale again you start all over.

The grand circle in meditation is visualized as a circle flowing through your body, connecting the center of spirit and the center of vital energy. In Taoist philosophy, the connection of these two psychic centers can have the power to heighten spirit, sensitivity, energy, and thought.

Creative Power in the Deep Meditative State: The "Ah Ha" Moment

Another aspect of Taoist meditation is the deep and vital creative state that can be attained. When we are in a deep meditative state, as in Taoist sitting meditation or T'ai Chi, we are in touch with our intuition. Millions of nerve cells from all areas of our brain are "firing" in synchronicity; that is, they are sending well-coordinated electric impulses to one another. Many parts of the brain are resonating, and the mind and body are acting as one. At such moments, we know instantly just what we should do. Suddenly we have the insight, the understanding, the intuition to do what is right. I call this point of discovery the "ah ha" moment.

There are many things you can do at such a moment. As a composer you can hear the exact musical piece you want to compose. As a singer you can have a new understanding of a particular song you sing, or you suddenly just know how to sing the song, so that you, the music, and the technique become one (see Chapter 7).

Although intuition, creativity, and inspiration are normal functions, we are usually not open, peaceful, or trusting enough for them to be expressed. Meditation and T'ai Chi are ways to help people achieve synchronicity and to be in touch with their intuition. It is important to have such inspirational moments, whether or not you are a performing artist.

Visualizing continuous circular movement in meditation and singing has helped me and others to produce free and good tones and to open up channels for expressive singing. In singing, your voice must unite with your energy, spirit, emotions, intuition, and thoughts. Vibrations produced by free and good tones and expressive singing can stimulate other vibrations, and lead your body and mind to a state of total harmony. Through continuous circular movement and sonic vibrations, it is possible to open up channels for us all to have those wonderful inspirational moments.

2

Taoist Philosophy in Singing and Breathing

Tao is unchanging as oneness, unceasing and ever-revolving.

LAO-TZU.

The Interplay of Opposite Forces and "Pulling In" the Sound

Those who live by Taoist philosophy aim at balancing every one of their actions. While singing, this concept should also apply. As your breath goes upward and out (yang), you should imagine that you are "pulling in" the sound (yin). Thinking that you are "pulling in"—which is of course directly opposite to your outgoing breath—applies the fundamental Taoist philosophy of the interplay of opposite forces. I have found that this technique helps to eliminate tension in the throat and helps the diaphragm to function properly without your having to control it consciously. It also creates focused energy behind your sound.

The concept of "pulling in" is based on three very important principles. The first, as we have been discussing, is the interplay of opposite forces; thus, when pulling in, you aim at maintaining a proper degree of mental and physical balance—neither relaxed nor tense—between you and an imaginary source. The object of this approach is to produce a totally balanced state of being. The second principle is continuous circular movement; thus, in the Pulling-In exercise, which will be explained shortly, you start and end a circle beginning from the center of spirit and moving toward the center of vital energy. The third principle is the belief in the importance of imagery and imagination, which can be used in singing in the same way they are used by a Chinese classical painter: Before putting the brush to the paper, the artist has already formed a clear picture in his or her mind's eye, through the force of imagination.

Over and over again in this book I will use such psychophysical techniques or phrases as *pull in* or *pulling in* the sound, accompanied by images or imaginary actions. (These are quite different from the usual physiological terms used, such as inhale.) For instance, I will ask you to imagine that your voice is as round, radiant, and warm as the sun; that your sound is chasing very fast after an imaginary ball, down toward the center of the Earth; or that you are embracing someone you love in order to re-create a glowing feeling. These images can stimulate you into a healthy, altered state of being, heightening your spirit and enabling you to re-create specific effects.

I remember that when I was a child in China I had a wonderful kite that my uncle made for me. We used to fly it together, and it was with him that I first understood the interplay of opposite forces. When flying the kite I learned that, whether my pull on the string was strong or gentle, I had to maintain a constant pull in order to have good control over the kite. The opposite force at work was the wind, which was always trying to blow the kite away from me. The strength of my pull on the string was determined by the strength of the wind and by whether I wanted the kite to come closer to me or move farther away, and at what speed. My uncle also advised me, "Pull the string as if you are pulling from the Tan-T'ien [center of vital energy]. Your pull will be stronger; you'll have more strength to control the kite."

The Pulling-In exercise is much the same. The procedure is to attach one end of a rope or string about eight feet long to a doorknob and then throw the other end over the top of the door, closing it so the rope will be anchored. Then stand about two feet away from the door, holding the string with your right hand in front of you and slightly above your forehead. Inhale while gently pulling in, as if you were flying a kite (see Figure 2). While doing so, you should imagine that you are pulling in toward your center of vital energy, about two inches below your navel. Your abdominal muscles will become firm and will automatically get your diaphragm to function properly. These are necessary conditions for good voice production.

Now you are ready to start singing. As you do so, first imagine that you pull in the sound against your outgoing breath, so that this pulling-in action travels through the center of spirit—between and behind your eyebrows—and then

FIGURE 2

down through your center of vital energy. You should imagine that your sound comes through these points, creating the first half of a smooth, continuous circular movement. You can apply the same approach in speaking, especially public speaking, or speaking your lines in a play when your voice is expected to be heard in a big hall.

In the following section, I will explain this exercise more fully, as it relates to continuous circular movement.

Exercises for Continuous Circular Movement

A smooth, continuous circular movement will assist the dynamic interplay of opposite forces and will help create the flowing vital energy required to produce a good strong sound or a soft lyrical one. It will also help you to control or coordinate your breath for singing or speaking without strain or rigidity, because your diaphragm will work effectively for you on its own. Here are some of the other benefits you will notice:

- You will not "punch" or "hit" a note or sound; instead you will have a smooth beginning to the sound.
- You will prevent the breath from rushing upward toward your throat and placing tension and pressure on your throat and vocal organ; instead your throat will be relaxed and your vocal cords will vibrate freely, producing a good sound.
- You will be able to use your breath actively, without rigidity, producing strong resonant or soft velvet sounds.
- You will be able to sing long notes or phrases or speak for a long period of time, especially without a microphone.

There are two directions for continuous circular movement to go in— vertical, which I use the most, and horizontal. The following are the steps to use for each exercise.

Vertical Circular Movement

1. While inhaling with your mouth open, raise your arm until your hand is in front of you and slightly above your forehead (Figure 3). At the same time, direct your breath by imagining that it goes to your center of vital energy, or Tan-T'ien. This area of your lower abdomen will then become firm.

2. Right after inhaling, imagine you are going to pull in the sound when you start to sing.

3. Start to sing as if the sound flows into you, simultaneously moving your hand downward to indicate the direction the sound is taking (Figure 4). When you practice this exercise often, you can actually feel the sound flowing into your head, your throat, your body, and your whole being. Concentrate on singing with an open throat (see Exercises for Opening the Throat, page 70).

4. Finish singing the note as though you are drawing it down toward your center of vital energy (Figure 5).

FIGURE 3   FIGURE 4

5. As you inhale to begin the next note, bring your arm upward again, as in step 1 (Figure 6).

Remember that the Vertical Circular Movement exercise only shows the direction of your sound, so you are not expected to make an actual perfect circle. In principle, you should use one large turn of vertical circular movement for a long note, and a small turn for a short note. For instance, suppose you have two accented short notes with one unaccented short note between them, such as in the phrase "*come* to *me*." Start your circle at the top, above your head, drawing the note downward while singing the word "come". Start the second half of the phrase at the bottom of the circle, turning and floating the note upward while singing on the unaccented word "to". Finish singing the phrase on the accented word "me" as you draw the note downward toward your center of vital energy. This will physically prevent you from punching the accented notes, an emphasisis resulting in tension in the throat and unpleasant sounds.

FIGURE 5

FIGURE 6

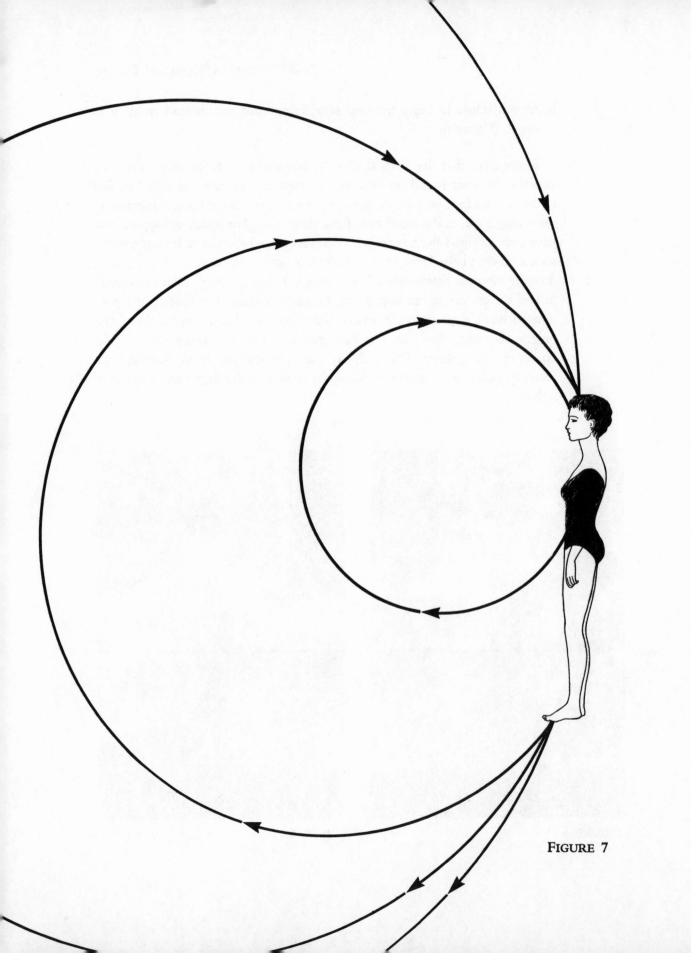

FIGURE 7

So, for long notes, use big circles; for short notes, use small circles. You can adapt the size and speed of the circular movement to your own need. The radius of the circle is not limited by the movement of your hand (see Figure 7). In your imagination, while doing this Vertical Circular Movement exercise, the size of the circle is unlimited; it can go up to heaven and deep down into the very center of the Earth! In fact, another way of finishing singing a long note is by imagining that the sound goes in a straight line deep into the Earth; singing in this way makes the voice sound very sturdy. You can also imagine that your sound, while traveling in circular movement, gathers and blends the wonderful vibrations of the sun, the universe, heaven, earth, ocean, nature, and people. When you think this way, your whole being will have richer vibrations.

Your tone sounds livelier and more vibrant when the imagined speed of movement of the circle is faster. In principle, the bigger the imagined circle, the faster the imagined speed. To create this vibrant sound, you can also imagine that your voice is chasing after a ball in a downward motion toward the center of the earth. As you gradually increase your vocal volume, simply imagine that you are chasing faster and faster after the ball.

In music, loud notes express heightened emotion. The use of this Vertical Circular Movement exercise not only helps you avoid getting tense due to this mounting energy, but also helps you keep your energy flowing.

While you are practicing singing and using your hand to direct the sound, make a point of using your left and right hands alternately, and sometimes both hands together.[1] After awhile, you can practice this exercise kinesthetically, that is, by imagining circular motion without actually using hand movements. Eventually, you will automatically feel your voice flowing in and out of you in circular movement.

Horizontal Circular Movement

1. Start this exercise by singing one long note, using the Vertical Circular Movement exercise described in the preceding pages. Begin on any note in your middle or medium-high range—wherever you feel comfortable and your throat does not get tight. (The higher notes are especially good for this exercise, as they will give you the most head resonance.) I suggest you use the round "ah" sound first; however, if you feel another vowel is better for you (e.g., the "ee" sound) then use it. If you prefer to use an initial consonant (e.g., "fah" or "mah"), go ahead. Sing your note at medium-loud volume for the first couple of minutes, then practice it louder. *You should practice with great enthusiasm, but do not force your voice.* This is one of the main Taoist principles.

FIGURE 8

2. Sustain your note while moving your hand in a rapid horizontal circle above your head, with fingers pointing downward (see Figure 8). As you do this, imagine your sound is in the form of a stream of radiant sunlight circling rapidly through the two hemispheres of your brain. While moving your

hand, move your arm with it, from the shoulder. As you will notice, while you are moving your hand quickly, your body will also automatically move with it, so don't worry if your sustained tone does not sound steady. When moving your right hand above your head, circle it in a counterclockwise direction. When using the left hand, circle it in a clockwise direction. Alternate the use of your right and left hands.

3. Hold your note until you feel you are about to run out of breath, but while you still feel energetic. Then inhale and continue.

Always avoid rigidity or tightness. For example, while holding the note, don't lock your jaw. Keep opening your upper throat. Hear the tone in your "mind's ear" before you sing it; don't worry about what may be wrong with the note that has already been sung. Think forward!

After practicing the Horizontal Circular Movement exercise for about five minutes, continue with it, but simply imagine the hand movements, mentally directing your voice to flow rapidly in continuous circular movement through the two hemispheres of your brain.

This exercise can help you increase the volume of your sound quickly. One night, after I had introduced this exercise to my students and they had practiced it together for a few minutes, someone knocked at the classroom door. I opened it, and a man said to me, "I teach a class in the next room. Your class is making very big sounds tonight. It is difficult for me to teach. Would you please try to keep the volume down?"

The Horizontal Circular Movement exercise can also help people to sing higher. One young male student of mine, although he used an open throat, could not sing higher than B♭ above middle C. After doing this exercise for a few minutes, he was able to sing a couple of notes higher.

Vertical Circular Movement and Horizontal Circular Movement are highly effective exercises for increasing vocal resonance in a short period of time. When students do these exercises for the first time, they can usually hear an obvious increase of resonance in the voice—the voice sounds bigger—even after practicing for only about ten minutes. They find this enjoyable and are motivated to practice some more. After doing these exercises for about fifteen minutes daily for a week or two, their voices gain even more resonance, and their awareness of resonance and its intensity increases.

It is important to point out that a student should work on other exercises for a short period of time before doing the circular movement exercises. These are the Pulling-In exercise in this chapter; the body movement and moving meditation exercises in Chapter 3; and, from Chapter 5, the exercises for good posture, open throat, adequate mouth opening, and good tones with proper inhaling.

It is also advisable that a student have a flexible, open throat and a good sense of the flow of energy while doing the Vertical Circular Movement exercise, before doing the Horizontal Circular Movement exercise. This usually takes about four to six weeks of practice.

The combined use of vertical and horizontal circular movement helps activate energy and stimulates the dynamic interplay of the left and right hemispheres of the brain. The voice, while creating good, free sonic vibrations, can stimulate the brain to operate at higher levels of energy, thus increasing an artist's creative potential.

3

Exercises Providing a Healthy Condition for Vocalizing and Performing

The secret of all natural and human law is movement that meets with
devotion . . . . Because enthusiasm shows devotion to movement,
heaven and earth are at its side and move with it.

I CHING

According to traditional practice, a singer is expected to vocalize before singing any song. Vocalizing is a warm-up exercise that aims to activate and coordinate the muscles and the breath for proper voice production.

The "mind-body-spirit" exercises presented in this chapter provide a healthy condition for vocalizing and performing as well as for creativity. They will free you from physical and emotional tension, clear your mind, heighten your energy, and lift your spirit. I suggest that you do these body movement exercises and Moving Meditation for at least ten minutes before beginning to sing. Of course, if you have more time it would be to your benefit to spend a little longer.

As you do these exercises, imagine that you are gathering in the wonderful vibrations of the universe. You move with this intention. Remember, you *are* a part of the universe, and the universe is a part of you. Let yourself be open to the vibration. Don't try hard, simply let it come to you. Let this feeling of freedom and openness flow into your vocalizing and singing. You should feel as though you are a child, open and uninhibited, full of enthusiasm and a great sense of fun.

Singing should become a part of your daily life. When you do these exercises often, you will see how much better you sing and how much more in harmony you are with Nature.

Before describing the exercises, I should say a word or two about music. You can do any of these exercises with or without music, depending on your personal feelings and preference. You may like complete silence, or perhaps to hear music in your imagination. When music is desired, I recommend selecting something gentle and lyrical. I do not use melancholy, syncopated, or chromatic music. You can choose appropriate movements from symphonies, concertos, sonatas, or other longer pieces; or use something shorter in its entirety.

Here are some pieces I use when I want something lively:

Beethoven: Symphony No. 6, "Pastoral Symphony" (first movement)

Smetana: "The Moldau"

Vangelis: "Chariots of Fire" (electronic music)

Vivaldi: "The Four Seasons" (Spring); Concerto in E for Violin, Strings, and Continuo (*allegro* movement)

When I want music that is gentle and lyrical, I often select one of the following:

Barber: Adagio for Strings

Beethoven: "Moonlight Sonata" (slow movement)

Chopin: Piano concertos (slow movements)

Copland: "Appalachian Spring"

Mozart: Piano Concerto No. 21 in C Major (second movement, *andante*)

Pachelbel: Canon in D

Sibelius: "The Swan of Tuonela"

Vangelis: "Ignatio" (first part) (electronic music)

Villa-Lobos: Bochianas Brasileiras No. 5 for Soprano and 8 Celli

Vivaldi: Concerto in E for Violin, Strings, and Continuo (*adagio* movement)

Occasionally I use certain Asian musical pieces, including Chinese, Indian, and Japanese selections. Kitaro's "Silk Road" and "Silk Road II" are recordings of synthesizer music with both gentle and lively pieces. I also use my own compositions, as well as my recordings of natural sounds such as the ocean, crickets, and singing birds. You can find commercial recordings in this latter area.

Over the last several years, with the development of synthesizers and other electronic instruments, a whole new area of sound has been created that is known as New Age music. I have mentioned only two artists in this area—Kitaro and Vangelis—although there are many more for you to explore.

Since music is very personal, it would be good for you to play pieces you like. Familiar ones are fine, but try also to listen to music by the masters that is not known to you. This will enrich your life by opening you up to new musical experiences.

Finally, you can also create new music and exercises for yourself, which can be a very rewarding experience.

Body Movement Exercises

Grand Solar Circle

1. Stand with your feet parallel to each other and apart a little more than shoulder width, your hands hanging comfortably at your sides (Figure 9).

FIGURE 9   FIGURE 10

2. Bring your hands together about two inches below your navel, palms over-lapping and facing up. Simultaneously squat down, with your heels on the ground, until the angle of your legs behind your knees is about 145° (Figure 10).

3. Keeping your hands together, raise your arms up over your head, making a wide arc in front of you, ending with your palms facing down. Inhale as you do this. Simultaneously straighten your legs and raise your heels until you are standing on your toes (Figure 11). Feel your arms and legs—indeed, your whole body—stretch with an open feeling. This and all movements should be done at a moderately slow speed.

4. As you gradually lower your heels to the ground, bring your hands downward again, in wide arcs to the sides, until they meet and overlap about two inches below the navel, as in step 2. Exhale as you do this (Figure 12). Again, simultaneously squat down, repeating steps 2 through 4.

Do the entire movement five or ten times, thinking to yourself, with enthusiasm, "I am collecting the wonderful vibrations of the universe," especially while lowering your arms. The motions you are making with your body

FIGURE 11

FIGURE 12

express this gathering in of energy. Notice yourself becoming stronger and more open and peaceful. Finish by lowering your hands sideways until your arms hang at the sides of your body.

Inhale and exhale through the nose, with the tip of your tongue resting on the front part of your hard palate. According to Taoist philosophy, you are connecting heaven and earth through you in this way. While inhaling, imagine your breath comes in through your center of spirit, a spot between and behind the eyebrows, then direct your breath to your center of vital energy, a spot about two inches below your navel, and notice how that area becomes firm. This is how deeply you should breathe when you sing or speak in a big hall. Speaking in conversations requires less firmness in this area.

Stretching My Wings

1. Stand with your feet parallel to each other and apart a little more than shoulder width, your hands hanging comfortably at your sides. Turn your upper body toward the right, at the same time raising your right arm in an arc to the side, with the palm facing downward (Figure 13). Inhale as you do this.

2. While gradually leaning down toward your left, lift your arm until it is at a 165° or so angle to your shoulder and your hand is pointing straight up, with the elbow slightly bent (Figure 14).

3. Exhaling, return your right arm to its original position while turning your upper body to the left. Now raise your left arm in the same way as you just did your right, inhaling and bending to the right (Figure 15).

4. As soon as your left hand is pointing straight up (Figure 16), return your left arm to its original position while exhaling and turning your upper body to the right, thus beginning the cycle over.

Do this series of movements—right and left—five times, all the while thinking to yourself, "I am stretching my wings like a big, beautiful bird." Take pleasure in the fluidity of your motions, the strength of your arms, and the opening up of your body while stretching. While inhaling and raising your arm, imagine your hand is drawing energy from the earth, heaven, and the universe, bringing it into your arm, lung, kidney, and leg on that side of your body, and back into the earth. Let your hand stay up until you complete this thought. After practicing this way for a few days or longer, you will feel energy going through the places in your body that you have imagined.

FIGURE 13

FIGURE 14

FIGURE 15

FIGURE 16

Simply Flying

1. Stand on your left leg, bending it slightly, and spread your arms sideways like a pair of wings, inhaling as you do. Stretch your right leg forward and exhale (Figure 17).

2. While inhaling, slowly lean your upper body forward and swing your right leg behind you, ending in the skaterlike position shown (Figure 18).

3. Holding your breath, straighten up; then swing your right leg forward again, exhaling. Do this movement forward and backward five times, always at a pace that is slow enough for you to maintain your balance easily.

4. Do the exercise five more times, standing on your right leg, with your left leg extending forward and backward.

As you perform these movements, think to yourself, "I am flying with joy." Notice how actively this exercise stimulates your center of vital energy and how well it centers and strengthens your life force. This exercise also puts your mind at rest because it demands your concentration. If you are thinking about other things besides inhaling and exhaling and directing the simple movements of your leg, you cannot balance yourself while doing this exercise.

FIGURE 17   FIGURE 18

Flapping My Wings

1. Stand with your feet apart at about shoulder width and the back of your left hand touching the palm of your right hand, held in front of your navel area. Squat down as low as is comfortable for you, as if about to sit in a chair (Figure 19).

2. With an upward thrusting motion, inhaling as you go, raise yourself up on your left leg to a standing position, while raising your right leg sideways as high as possible and simultaneously spreading your arms outward and upward like a pair of wings. Touch them above your head, palms down, with the right palm over the back of the left hand (Figure 20).

3. Exhaling, lower your hands and leg to their starting positions (Figure 21). Do this movement five times, alternating your standing leg.

While doing this exercise, imagine that you are an angel or a big, beautiful bird flapping your wings. Allow your natural enthusiasm to come through, so you become open and uninhibited, playful like a child. This exercise is good for activating your energy, especially the breath energy that comes from the center of vital energy.

FIGURE 19   FIGURE 20   FIGURE 21

~~~~~

Soothing My Back

1. Stand with your feet parallel to each other and apart a little more than shoulder width, with your hands on your waist. Bend at the knees slightly, to form an approximate 145° angle behind the knees (Figure 22).

2. Keeping your rib cage steady and centered, rotate your hips in a circle from left to right (Figures 23, 24, 25). Keep the movement slow and smooth, inhaling quietly while the hips circle behind you. Sense the breath flowing into your lower back as you inhale; you will feel your lower back expand a little with this thought. Think with a smiling feeling, "I am soothing my lower back."

3. Each set of hip rotations consists of five circles from left to right and five circles from right to left. Complete two or three sets in each practice, before moving on to the next exercise.

Doing this exercise several times a day will relax your back and open the energy flow in your spinal column. To further the benefit of this excellent exercise, raise your arms to the side and touch fingertips to shoulders. Bend at the knees and proceed as directed above. This will take you one step further in easing tension in the back and head. In addition to being a prerequisite for good health, maintaining a continuous and unforced energy flow is vital to helping the voice produce rich sounds.

FIGURE

FIGURE 24

FIGURE 25

Orbiting Around the Sun

1. Stand with your feet apart a little more than shoulder width, knees slightly bent, hands resting at your sides (Figure 26). Imagine you are standing right above a warm, radiant sun. You are much bigger than life, and much bigger than this sun, which is about the size of a soccer ball, relative to you.

2. Bend forward from the hips to about a ninety-degree angle, with your eyes looking at the ground. In this position pretend you are holding a long pole between your hands (Figure 27).

FIGURE 26

FIGURE 27

FIGURE 28

3. Bring the imaginary pole around to your right side (Figure 28). Inhaling, turn it and raise it up over your head, leaning backward as you do (Figure 29). Exhaling, bring the pole down to the left side and around once again to the front (Figures 30 and 31). As you make this circle with your arms, you will make a horizontal circle with your hips.

Do this circle five times, from right to left, then five times from left to right. As you do these movements, imagine you are rotating around the sun, with a feeling of fun. While you are turning the pole around, imagine that your hips are also rotating around the sun. This exercise helps you to feel the expansiveness of your being and that you have a warm, energetic feeling within you.

FIGURE 29   FIGURE 30   FIGURE 31

―――――――――――――――――――――― ∽∾∽∾

Golden Rooster Standing on One Leg

1. Stand erect with your legs together. Maintain a flexible, relaxed feeling, and don't lock your knees. Look forward with soft eyes, without staring (Figure 32).

2. Inhale smoothly while raising your right leg and right arm simultaneously at a moderately slow speed. Raise your thigh to a horizontal position, with your knee forming a right angle; at the same time raise your arm to form a right angle at the elbow, with your middle fingertip at the level of your eyebrows (Figure 33). Your thumb should be toward you and your palm should face left.

3. Start to pull downward in a circular movement (Figure 34). Exhale smoothly as you move your hand down and lower your leg until your foot is flat on the floor again.

4. As soon as your right foot is on the floor, begin to inhale and raise your left leg and arm, as you finish lowering your slightly bent right arm back down to your side. Repeat the movement with the left leg and arm.

Do this exercise at least five times on each side, alternating sides continuously. You can do it more times, for as long as you feel comfortable, especially if you are doing it as a separate activity. Remember to do this exercise at a moderately slow speed, using the proper breathing. This movement, which is an adaptation of a T'ai Chi exercise, is very good for centering yourself, deepening your breathing, and generating your vital energy. It also helps to dissolve tension. Enjoy the flowing feeling of the movement.

FIGURE 32

FIGURE 33

FIGURE 34

Moving Meditation

This exercise is also a modified version of a T'ai Chi form, developed in China in the thirteenth century.

1. Stand erect without tension, with your feet apart at about shoulder width, toes pointed forward. Let your torso rest comfortably on your hip sockets. Let your hands stay relaxed by the sides of your body. Look ahead with soft eyes. Exhaling gently, lower your body by bending your knees a bit, without strain, to form about a 145° angle behind the knees (Figure 35).

2. Remaining relaxed, bring your arms forward very slightly and bend them at the elbows until your fingertips are at shoulder height. Your palms should be facing outward. At the same time, begin to straighten your legs, inhaling as you go up (Figure 36).

3. When your hands are up and your legs are almost straight, start to lower your body again by bending your knees, exhaling as you go down. At the same time, pull your elbows back and lower your hands to your sides (Figure 37). By this time your knees should once again be bending to about 145°.

4. Repeat the movement by repeating steps 2 and 3.

Do this exercise ten times, smoothly, slowly, and comfortably, with a flowing feeling of constant speed. When you bend your knees, do so only to the point where it still feels easy to come back up. When doing your arm movements, start and end with slightly bent arms and move them as if in a continuous circular motion. As the arms rise higher and higher, the elbows naturally bend more until they gradually form angles of about ninety degrees.

Remember to inhale while going up and exhale while coming down. While inhaling, imagine the breath going down to your center of vital energy. As your arms and body start to move upward, you will feel this Tan-T'ien area getting firm (not tight), which is how you should feel when you inhale for singing, whether sitting or standing. While exhaling, you may just let your breath energy flow with the movement, or you may imagine your hands are very gently pressing the air down.

Moving Meditation is a simple and effective exercise utilizing the continuous circular movement of the hands and arms. It helps you to breathe deeply in a relaxed way, generate unforced energy flow, and center and ground yourself.

It is also beneficial for people who are interested in practicing meditation without sitting still. If you do this exercise purely for meditation purposes, there should be no limit on how long you practice it; however, make sure you do not tire yourself out. Give yourself a short rest between sets of twenty or thirty.

FIGURE 35

FIGURE 36

FIGURE 37

4

Thirty Essential
Vocal Exercises

What a joy it is to learn and to practice consistently.

CONFUCIUS

Exercise is part of a whole. Exercise expertly performed is the foundation for a beautiful and expressive performance.

ANONYMOUS

Applying Taoist Principles

In this chapter I present a series of thirty essential vocal exercises, which I use as the fundamentals in teaching the Tao of voice to my students. These exercises are designed and practiced according to the following principles.

- Since the Taoist principle of the interplay of opposite elements is paramount in this technique, these exercises make use of various opposites such as loud and soft, fast and slow, high and low, and *staccato* and *legato*.

- In keeping with the Taoist principle of using things in their natural state, the natural inflections of speech patterns such as loud and soft are applied to training. Thus, in vocal music as in speech, we don't produce every word or every syllable with equal loudness; the important words or accented syllables sound louder and/or higher.

- Since freedom and flexibility are considered to be natural states of being, these exercises activate the flexible movement of the diaphragm and abdominal muscles and the free flow of breath energy for singing. This is done through practicing loud and soft tones, sung with a wide range of dynamics.

- In order to realize the full potential of each singer's voice, four essential types of exercises are used to extend vocal range and dynamics. The first three are scales, arpeggios, and sustained tones; the fourth involves combinations of these.

- Taoist philosophy cautions against the use of force, as it produces tension and rigidity. These activities are thus designed to prevent rigidity by stimulating and creating a feeling of flexibility in your body, throat, and whole being, through the interplay of opposite forces and continuous circular movement. The latter is coordinated with vocal exercises and singing.

- Practice the exercises regularly, but don't overdo it. Do what you feel you need most first.

- The important Taoist concept of maintaining a nonstrenuous, flowing energy level while relaxing is highlighted in these exercises and should be applied while practicing or performing. Observing this in daily life is also of great benefit.

General Instructions

BRINGING THE EXERCISES TO LIFE

A vocal exercise does not simply consist of a series of notes; it is brought to life by expressing emotions. So let your imagination, emotion, intuition, and energy flow; let your whole being glow and dance. In so doing, you will transform each of the exercises in this chapter.

Once you have learned Exercise 1, do all subsequent exercises with the first one in mind. Exercise 1 is the best illustration of how to apply continuous circular movement to singing. Once you have become familiar with it, you will find it easy to apply to the other exercises, with only minor adjustments. Special instructions for those who cannot sing the five-note scale can be found on page 51.

For example, when you apply continuous circular movement to various exercises, pay attention to the loudness and the length of notes. In some exercises, one loud note is followed by a soft note; in others, one loud note is followed by two or more soft notes. As described in Chapter 2, it is important to remember that when you sing a loud note your hand is at the top of the circle, coming down toward you or pulling in the sound while you are singing. As your hand is going out and upward in the circle, you sing the soft note or notes that follow the loud note.

As for the length of notes, usually one long note needs one big circle. When the long note is the last note of a phrase, however, or is one note by itself, you end the note by pulling in the sound as your hand comes off the top of the circle, down toward you. You imagine that you are directing the note to your center of vital energy. In other words, you do not complete the whole circular hand movement, but rather end it at that first half of the circle. If the first or last note is soft, pull in the sound in this way as well.

The terms *loud* and *soft* (often abbreviated as "L" or "S") as used in these vocal exercises simply indicate that one note is slightly louder than the other. These dynamics are relative; therefore, you don't strictly have to sing loudly and softly. You may sing a loud note as moderately loud and a soft one as moderately soft. In fact, it is better for your voice at first if you sing all the loud notes as moderately loud. After your voice has warmed up, or when your voice is getting stronger, you may sing very loud, as long as your voice is not strained. (See Table 1 in Chapter 5 for a listing of the Italian terms that are used in music to indicate these dynamic levels, if you are not already familiar with them. They are used on the scores in this chapter.)

Sing the notes marked "soft" as moderately soft, soft, or very soft, depending, again, on the degree of softness in the ending of the preceding note. In principle, just sing the soft note almost as soft as the ending of the preceding note. In some cases, a soft note may be sung as moderately loud, if its preceding note was sung loud or very loud.

In order to move smoothly from a loud to a soft note, sing the ending of the loud note with gradually decreasing loudness. There are a number of notes in these vocal exercises marked to be sung gradually louder ($<$) and softer ($>$). These dynamics are known as crescendos and decrescendos. Practicing such dynamics will not only help you move from one note to another smoothly (harmoniously, in the Taoist sense), it will also help you sing with expression and finesse.

Continuous circular movement and breathing, together with the techniques for opening the throat described in Chapter 5, will make it easier for you to learn to sing gradually louder and gradually softer, and to do all the exercises with excellent results. Of course, you will have to practice with faith, discipline, and regularity, as well as enthusiasm.

Since learning a technique requires mental and physical repetition, it will do you good to review often the material in the other chapters of this book, related to these exercises.

Sing the exercises with or without words. You may vocalize them with "ah" or "aw" first, then with other vowels or vowels preceded by a variety of consonants. Practice them in various keys.

Be inventive. You may find it helpful and stimulating to create your own exercises. Or, you may find that certain phrases in a particular song or aria bring out the good quality of your voice, or cause problems that need to be solved. You may take these on as exercises. It can be fun to share your variations and original creations with others.

PRONUNCIATION OF VOWELS

The sound of the voice is carried by vowels, so it is necessary for you to sing with good vowel sounds. Vocalize on the following vowels, which are the basic ones widely used by singers and teachers when doing vocal exercises.

"Ah," as in "father."

This vowel gives you the widest space at the back of your mouth, helping you to develop and feel your open throat, as well as to sense the roundness of a tone. It is considered to be a "workhorse" vowel. You should imagine that the "ah" sound is as round as the radiant sun. (Make sure that the "ah" sound, as well as the "aw," "oh," and "oo" vowels to be discussed shortly, do not turn into an "uh" sound.)

"Aw," as in "law."

This vowel lends a little more warmth to a sound and tends to keep the sound closer to a round tone. If your "ah" is lacking in roundness or warmth, try to hear the vowel "aw" in your mind's ear; it will help you.

"Oh," as in "toe" and "rose."

This vowel should be sung as the diphthong[1] "oh-oo," ending on "oo" as in "too." Make sure you don't accentuate the "oo" sound; just let it flow from the "oh" sound.

"Oo," as in "too."

Compared to other vowels, this one has more depth and a more concentrated sound. It helps you to sense the depth of your sound as well as to focus your tone. It is good to use this vowel as a lead-up to the "ee," "ay," and "eh" vowels, when these sound thin.

"Eh," as in "men" and "there."

In order to get a round sound for this vowel, think of the "ir" sound (as in "bird," without the "r"), or the French "eu."

"Ay," as in "way."

Also a diphthong, this vowel ends on an "ee" sound. As with other diphthongs, don't accentuate the second sound; let the "ee" flow smoothly from the long "a" sound, at the end of the note.

"Ee," as in "see" or "tea."

This is the brightest vowel. Avoid spreading your lips, as this tends to make "ee" sound thin or piercing. You can produce a round "ee" sound by vocalizing with "oo," by adding "*w*" to make "wee," or by thinking of the French "u" sound, as in "tu." In other words, you sing "oo-ee."

Though there are other vowels, they are closely related to one of these seven basic ones and can be vocalized in the same way.

PRONUNCIATION OF CONSONANTS

Since words consist of consonants as well as vowels, it is important for you to vocalize using consonants along with vowels. The basic consonants for vocal exercises include *b, d, f, h, l, m r, s,* and *v,* plus *w* and *y,* which are actually part consonant and part vowel.

M.

People start to use *m* when they are babies. Usually our first word is *mama*. This consonant can add resonance to the vowels. However, if your voice tends to sound nasal, avoid using *m* at first, as well as *n* and *ng*.

R.

For the purpose of vocalizing, use the rolled *r*, as the British and Italians do. Let the tip of your tongue roll once or twice on the front part of your hard palate.

This *r* will help you to develop the flexibility of your tongue and to focus your breath energy.

F and H.

Both consonants, especially *h*, activate the diaphragm, the abdominal muscles, and the breath energy. When you practice using "fah" or "ha" (as if you are laughing), you will find that your spirits will be elevated.

W.

The consonant *w* helps to bring roundness to the vowels, as in "we," "want," "way," "well," and "willow."

Y.

A dull tone can be turned into a bright one with the help of *y*. If any of your vowel sounds are dull, practice them with *y* preceding them, as in "yah," "yaw," and "yoh."

The combinations that can be made with consonants and vowels are numerous. Sometimes you or your teacher must find combinations that can help you solve your specific problems. Unless you have an acute or very special difficulty, there will be enough combinations using the consonants and vowels just listed for you to practice on.

One simple way to work with consonants is try to keep your open throat flexible and to keep your teeth apart, whether or not the consonants bring your lips together. You should also try to get consonants out of the way quickly, that is, finish singing them as soon as you can.

CHOOSING THE BEST KEY AND TEMPO FOR PRACTICING

Most of the exercises that are provided in this book are written in the key of C, although some are written in two keys. If this key doesn't suit your vocal range, transpose it to one that is more appropriate. For an exercise that uses two different keys, practice in one key until you are familiar with it and then do it in the other. You can also transpose it by half steps downward and upward. Go as low and as high as you like, as long as your voice is not strained.

Regarding tempo, the exercises should be done moderately slow at first (except where a specific tempo is indicated), and then faster, and then slower.

Exercises

Exercise 1

Exercise 1 is for singing with continuous circular movement, using your hand to guide you and activate your imagination. It was described previously, in Chapter 2, as the Vertical Circular Movement exercise.

Alternate the use of your left and right hand to direct continuous circular movement. Later on you will not need your hands, as you will be able to imagine the movement, or experience it kinesthetically. You should then alternate the kinesthetic movement with the real movement. After practicing for a period of time, you will use the real movement less and less, until eventually the movement will become part of you. Your singing will automatically flow with continuous circular movement.

When inhaling, focus on the pointers given in Chapter 5, in the section entitled "Producing Good Tones by Proper Inhaling." As you begin to sing, imagine that you are pulling in the sound through the center of spirit, simultaneously opening your throat and mouth a little more, with a welcoming feeling. The sound you are singing is being pulled in, using continuous circular movement. When you finish the first note, you should be halfway through the circle. The second note is sung while your hand is in the second half of the continuous circular movement, beginning as your hand begins going upward. Start the third note on the beginning of another round, just as you sang the first note, again pulling it in. The fourth note is sung the same way as the second note. As you move to the fifth note, you begin the third circle, once again pulling in the note. End the note while your hand is *still* pulling in on the first half of the third circle. At this point you should feel that your center of vital energy and the lower back are becoming slightly firm, but not rigid.

Take care not to "hit" the loud notes. Instead, start them at *mezzo forte* and pull them in so the initial moment of each note is not loud. This will help prevent a harsh sound. As you are singing a loud note, decrease the volume smoothly, so you move from note to note smoothly. When singing soft notes, don't sing too softly. Start with *mezzo piano*, almost as soft as the ending of the preceding note. As a general rule, open your throat and mouth more for loud and high notes, and a little less for low and soft notes.

Throughout these exercises, the straight line following a syllable or vowel indicates how long you should sustain that sound. For instance, in the following exercise the syllable "mah" is sustained for the notes G and F, then repeated and sustained for the notes E and D, and again repeated on the C note. "Aw" is sustained through all five notes.

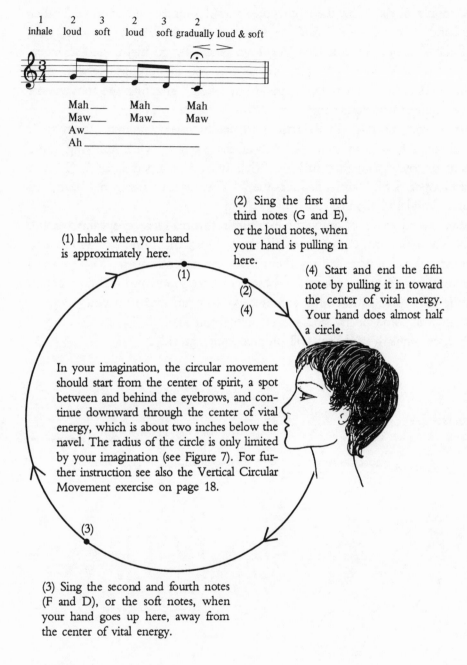

1	2	3	2	3	2
inhale	loud	soft	loud	soft	gradually loud & soft

Mah___   Mah___   Mah
Maw___   Maw___   Maw
Aw_____
Ah _____

(1) Inhale when your hand is approximately here.

(2) Sing the first and third notes (G and E), or the loud notes, when your hand is pulling in here.

(4) Start and end the fifth note by pulling it in toward the center of vital energy. Your hand does almost half a circle.

In your imagination, the circular movement should start from the center of spirit, a spot between and behind the eyebrows, and continue downward through the center of vital energy, which is about two inches below the navel. The radius of the circle is only limited by your imagination (see Figure 7). For further instruction see also the Vertical Circular Movement exercise on page 18.

(3) Sing the second and fourth notes (F and D), or the soft notes, when your hand goes up here, away from the center of vital energy.

Those of you who cannot sing the five-note scale in Exercise 1 at the moment can simply sing on one note, following the instructions here and using only the sound "mah." Repeat "mah" five times in one breath. Hold each note a couple of seconds. Don't accent any of them. You can practice with the "mah" sound for a couple of days and then use other vowel sounds, and even add other consonants. Use "ah" or "mah" to start the exercise. Practice within your comfortable range, but don't start too low. Gradually go higher and stronger.

You can also sing a very simple, familiar tune you are comfortable with, such as "Jingle Bells" or "Twinkle, Twinkle Little Star," adapting the movements and breathing to fit your song.

When you are able, do Exercise 1 for about twenty minutes, then walk around for a couple of minutes. Repeat the exercise while thinking some pleasant or joyful thoughts, such as, "Oh, what a wonderful day," "I see a beautiful open sky," "Someone loves me," "There is sunshine in my heart," or "I have wonderful friends."

After several weeks of doing the exercise in this manner, try speaking aloud, to the same rhythm, "Happy life is now." Hold the important words and accented syllables longer and say them louder, with enthusiasm. You will feel your voice has a better, stronger, and more mellow sound and will flow better. Use the same process for other expressions. You can make up your own, or you can read some poems and speeches that you like.

Practice regularly and you will progress quite quickly.

Exercise 2A

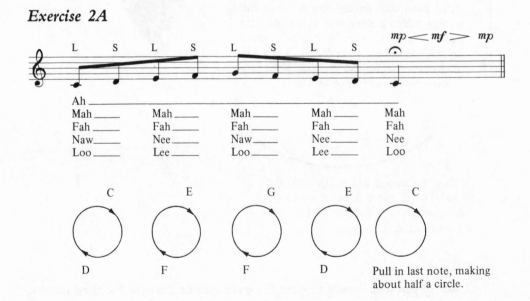

Exercise 2B

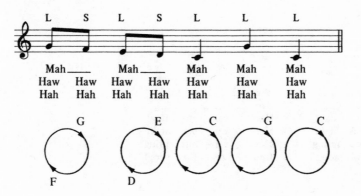

Sing "haw" and "hah" as if you are delightfully surprised.

Exercise 3

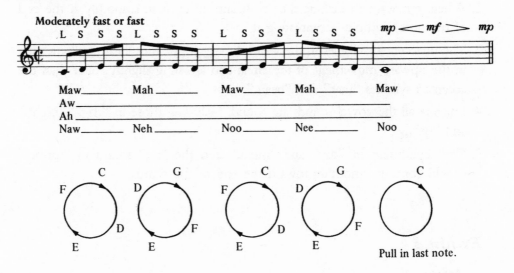

Try also using "hah" for every note, and feel as if you are laughing slightly. Make sure your throat is not tight. You don't need to go higher than E (the fourth space), unless your voice can go higher without strain.

Exercise 4

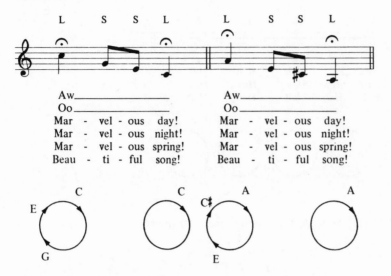

1. Sing "mar" in "marvelous" as "mah," without the "r" sound.

2. When you want to include the "r" sound, bring it in smoothly at the end of the note, without accentuating it.

3. The unaccented syllables in the words "mar<u>vel</u>ous" and "beau<u>tiful</u>" are sung in the upward movement of the circle and are sung slightly softer than the accented syllables "mar" and "beau."

4. Imagine all the vowel sounds are round, including those in "d<u>ay</u>," "n<u>i</u>ght," and "spr<u>ing</u>."

5. The diphthongs in "day" and "night," and the "ng" sound in "spring," should come in smoothly toward the end of the words.

Exercise 5

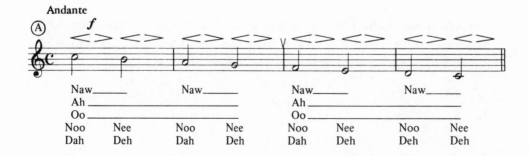

Ⓑ

Ah Eh Ee Aw Oo   Ah Eh Ee Aw Oo   *(Repeat the syllables)*
Aw Eh Ee Oh Ah   Aw Eh Ee Oh Ah
Oo Ee Eh Aw Ah   Oo Ee Eh Aw Ah

Complete one circle for each long note (♩) except the last note (C). Pull in the last note, making half a circle.

Use the vowel sounds "ah," "eh," "ee," "aw," and "oo." You can add consonants such as "d," "m," "n," "s," and others preceding the vowel sounds, and add the rolled "r" to the end of the vowel sounds. Use all of these sounds for Exercises 6–8 as well.

Exercise 6

Exercise 7

Exercise 8

Exercise 9

Hah Hah Hah Hah Hah Hah Hah Hah
Prah Pree Prah Pree Prah Pree Prah Pree

Sing "hah" with a joyful feeling. Use the rolled "r" here. Additional sounds to use are "haw," "hoo," and "fah." The "h" sound is very good for activating your center of vital energy and your diaphragm, and it helps to activate the tone. "F" also helps.

Exercise 10*

The following exercise uses *staccato*, and Exercise 11 uses a combination of *staccato* with a sustained note and *legato*. Both are very good for developing flexibility, agility, and free production of the voice.

Sing this on "ah" or "aw"; then try "hah" or "haw," imagining you are laughing lightly. Make sure your throat is not tight, because laughing tends to tighten the throat.

Exercise 11*

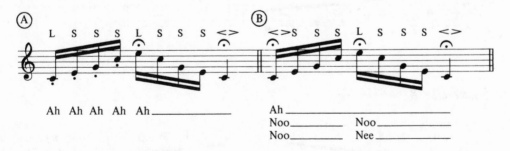

Ah Ah Ah Ah Ah_____

Ah _____
Noo_____ Noo_____
Noo_____ Nee _____

*When you are comfortable in doing A, then do B.

Exercise 12*

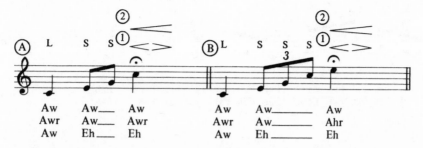

You can also sing this on "yaw," "ah," "ahr," "yah," and "eh" or "fee." For "awr" and "ahr," use a rolled Italian "r." This will help your breath energy continue to flow and will improve the flexibility of your tongue. Do the two exercises for a couple of minutes.

Exercise 13*

Vocalize exercise A using each of the syllables shown in exercise B. Sustain one syllable for two notes. This exercise helps to bring a lively or bright sound to low notes.

Exercise 14*

This exercise helps to increase the depth of the sound of high notes and to enrich their resonance.

---

*When you are comfortable in doing A, then do B.

Exercise 15

Ah or Aw

| Fah Feh Fee Fah Feh Fee | Fah Feh Fee Fah Feh Fee | Fah |
| Fee Feh Fah Fee Feh Fah | Fee Feh Fah Fee Feh Fah | Fee |

Exercise 16

Aw

Sing this on "aw," "ah," "oo," "fee," or "feh."

Exercise 17

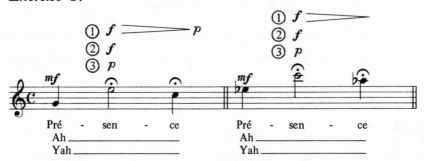

Pré - sen - ce   Pré - sen - ce
Ah _____   Ah _____
Yah _____   Yah _____

I have found the French word *présence* (it means presence) is very good in helping me to get my high C. The nasal sound of "sen" disappears when it is sung on a high note and instead gains a ringing quality. It is possible that the consonants *p* and rolled *r* help to activate the breath energy, and the interval of the sixth helps the high notes sound with a more ringing quality through drawing some rich resonance in the medium high notes. If you feel the French vowel sound "é" in "pré" is not comfortable for you to do, use "preh" as in the English word "presence." Sing the low note here *mezzo forte*, and sing the ending of this note slightly softer but without letting your energy sag. Then take in the high note without delay. You don't have to go to high C, nor must you stop there. Go as high as you can, as long as your voice is not strained.

Exercise 18

This is another interval for you to use in reaching your high notes, as is the one given in Exercise 19. Some singers feel that the vowels "aw" and "ih" (as in "in") help them to get to high notes more easily. Others feel "ah" is better, especially for notes higher than G above the staff.

Exercise 19

Use the same vowel sounds as in Exercise 18.

Exercise 20

Vocalize this exercise using the syllables "fah" and "feh." Then use "m" and "d" as consonants, and vocalize on "mah," "meh," "dah," and "deh."

Exercise 21

For Exercises 21–23, vocalize with "aw" first. Then use "ah," "oo," "eh," and "ih" (as in "in"). "Aw" is a more mellow sound than "ah," and "oo" is very good for focusing your sound. "Eh" and "ih" are brighter sounds. Use the pattern of a louder note followed by one or two (Exercise 22) softer notes throughout, as indicated.

Exercise 22

This exercise and the next two are very good for developing the fluidity, flexibility, and strength of the voice.

Exercise 23

Exercise 24

This segment is taken from the tenor aria "Every Valley," in the "Messiah," by Handel. The original key is E.

Exercise 25

Exercise 26

Exercise 27

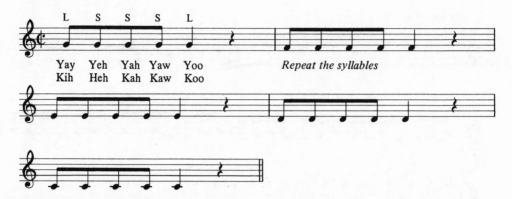

Yay Yeh Yah Yaw Yoo
Kih Heh Kah Kaw Koo

Repeat the syllables

This exercise trains you to sing *y* and *k* with flexibility. You don't need to go higher than the fourth space (E). Keep the tempo energetic.

Exercise 28

Sing this on "ah" or "hah."

Exercise 29

Oo_____
Foo_____ Foo
Ah _____

Oo_____
Foo_____ Foo
Ah _____

This exercise helps you to sing chromatic scales.

Exercise 30

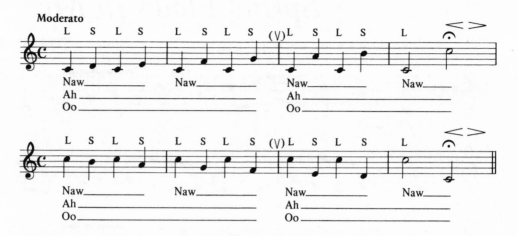

This exercise helps you to sing frequently used intervals.

A Song Without Words

Spring Flows in Me

I wrote this song to express my warm feelings about spring, using music and no words. When I sing this, I treat my voice as an instrument. Written mostly in a pentatonic scale, this song is especially good for *legato* singing.

Sing this piece on "ah" or "aw." Sing moderately slow, with a warm and flowing feeling.

In principle, the notes on the downbeats should be sung slightly louder than those on the upbeats; in a group of two notes, or three or four notes, the first note of the group is sung slightly louder. Examples:

Spring Flows in Me was given its world premiere by flutist Carol Wincenc at the Peace Bell Ceremony and Concert for Peace, held at the United Nations on Earth Day, March 20, 1991.

Spring Flows In Me

Andante, with a warm and bright feeling

Music by **STEPHEN CHUN-TAO CHENG**

You may sing the high C instead of the C as notated in the last bar of
either of the endings.

*Bar 55: Alternative melodic line.

All the grace notes in this song should
be sung softer than the main notes.

5

Techniques for Beginning Students

Tao is like a flowing river.

LAO TZU

While the emphasis in this chapter is on basic techniques for beginning singers, those who are studying voice production for the purposes of speaking will also find many of them useful. Since the speaking voice usually does not need to extend beyond the chest register, and commonly moves between the medium-low and low ranges of the voice, those of you wishing to develop your speaking voice can practice the open-throat exercises and other exercises that do not emphasize developing high notes or do not involve much music.

However, it would be beneficial to extend your vocal range a little beyond your chest register into your head register. The famous British actor Sir John Gielgud had a rich vocal range, and often marked his script with many terms used to note dynamics and tempo in music scores. These marks would remind him, for example, to speak certain lines loud or soft, fast or slow, gradually louder or softer, gradually faster or slower, or suddenly very loud or soft. When you can learn to use your voice in this way, and let it flow through the fullness of your vocal range, your voice will be more interesting and effective.

The Importance of Good Posture

Before you do any exercises, it is important to have good posture. According to Taoist practice, good posture is not only essential for appearance, it is also necessary for the free flow of breath and vital energy, which is absolutely necessary for singing. The following are some pointers.

- Stand erect. Maintain a straight line, or an approximately straight line, from the crown of your head, through your chest, to your lower abdomen.
- Relax your shoulders; let them drop.
- Feel your torso resting comfortably on your hip sockets.
- Hold your chest in its natural erect position. Don't slump, but don't pull back your shoulders, either. You should have a sense of well-being, ease, and openness.
- When you are inhaling, your lower abdomen—the center of vital energy—should expand only slightly. You should feel that your waistline and lower back are also expanding. Always try to maintain a feeling of flexibility.
- Keep your knees flexible; do not lock them.
- For a resilient posture, alternate putting your weight on the ball of each foot. One foot should be slightly ahead of the other, with a little space between them. Don't sink back on your heels.
- Look ahead with relaxed eyes; do not stare.
- Let your arms hang loosely at your sides; your hands, wrists, and fingers should be relaxed as well.
- Avoid raising or dropping your head, or turning it sideways. If you need to turn your head, turn your whole body with it.
- If you use your hands while vocalizing or singing a song, hold them above waist level, as you do when you talk.
- When you sing in a classical concert, your hands and body movements should be less animated than if you are singing in a pop concert, cabaret, or opera.
- If you feel your back is getting tight or rigid, take a little bow, or a couple of little bows, and breathe smoothly.
- If you are singing while sitting down, lean forward slightly and let your shoulders drop. Maintain a straight back without feeling rigid. Place both feet comfortably, flat on the ground; do not cross your legs.

• When you are portraying a character in a play, there will be certain variations to your posture, such as when you have to lie down. Under all circumstances, be aware of your body; do not let yourself get tense or rigid, especially in the areas of your neck and back.

Exercises for Opening the Throat

A flexible, open throat is essential for producing good, ringing tones. An open throat provides a smooth passage through which air can freely travel, and space for the sound to resonate well. An open throat helps to extend vocal range and dynamics, and it enables you to breathe more deeply in less time and to use less breath when singing.

The open area at the back of the mouth is where the resonance of the voice is produced.[1] It consists of the nasal pharynx, the oral pharynx, and the laryngeal pharynx, all of which are adjustable resonators that together form a space where the vibrating air can oscillate.

An open throat creates more physical space for sound. When the soft palate—the back part of the roof of your mouth—is raised and the uvula attached to it is lifted, the throat is more open. (The uvula is the fleshy lobe hanging at the back of the soft palate. The ancient Chinese called it Tiaochung, or the "hanging bell," probably because they discovered that when the "hanging bell" was raised the voice would be more resonant.) When your throat is opened properly, there should be a feeling of openness and flexibility, especially at the back of your mouth. Your jaw, tongue, and lips should also be flexible and relaxed.

When you wish to practice opening this passageway, it is useful to imagine your throat as a very large personal universe. Imagine that the top of your universe opens to receive the wonderful vibrations from the infinite universe around you. You will feel more energized, and much bigger than life. You will feel your voice flowing with strength and energy as the vibrations from the universe around you blend with those vibrations from your own being.

The following five exercises are ways to open the throat.

About to Yawn

Allow yourself to feel as though you are about to yawn, while making the round vowel "ah" sound. By doing this you will find that your throat automatically opens much more than usual, especially the back of your mouth.

Meanwhile, your jaw will also open up automatically. Make sure that it drops enough so that if you place your index finger at the jaw joint—in front of and adjacent to your ear—you can feel a significant, small indentation. If you do not, you have not opened your jaw and throat enough.

The opening of the throat at the back of the mouth and the dropping of the jaw should be the result of the about-to-yawn feeling. Be sure not to try to push your jaw down. Also remember that you are *not* actually yawning, since yawning tightens the throat. The about-to-yawn feeling is very different.

This is the best exercise I know for opening the throat quickly. It is also very helpful when you are singing a high note. Open your upper throat a little more, using the about-to-yawn feeling, and you will be surprised at how easily you can sing the high note!

Siren Sound

Begin by imagining you are about to pull in your sound through the region between and behind your eyebrows, the center of spirit. Imagine that this sound will move down through your throat, toward your center of vital energy below your navel. As you imagine this, start a soft, falling siren sound, beginning as high as you comfortably can, on the round vowel "ah." You should use the about-to-yawn feeling when beginning this sound. Try to hear the sound clearly in your mind's ear before you start to sing it. As your siren sound comes down from your head register to your chest register, you should focus on stretching the back of your upper throat more and more. Men can start the siren sound with a falsetto which, sounding like a female voice, can also help to create an open throat. The falsetto will flow into the real voice smoothly and without a voice break when you bring in the real voice with a soft sound. Welcome the siren sound into your whole being. If you feel a strain in your throat, open it a little less. You should also not strain your throat by letting the sound go too low or too high.

A round "ah" sound helps more than any other vowel sound to create a large open space at the back of the mouth. While practicing the Siren Sound exercise, beginners usually have the tendency of letting "ah" change into "uh" when coming down to the lower register. Be sure to keep a round "ah" sound all the time, and don't let your throat close up. As you come down into the lower register you may sometimes notice that your sound is scattered. To focus your voice, keep your lower lip barely covering your teeth and don't open the mouth too wide.

Sometimes when you sing a song that requires you to shift your voice from your head register to your chest register, or vice versa, a break occurs in your voice. It appears as an abrupt change of color or quality in the voice. The Siren Sound exercise is the best method I know to help you get rid of this break and to even out the change in quality. Work on pulling in the sound more gently and softly as you approach the approximate breaking point. At the same time, don't let your energy sag. The Siren Sound exercise helps to link sounds smoothly so that you don't concentrate on each individual note. Because of this you can glide naturally over the voice break without stumbling over it and so get rid of it quickly and easily.

At any time, but especially when you are first beginning to learn to do the Siren Sound exercise, you might feel that, when pulling in the sound, you are not getting the good, smooth sound you want when going from your high to low registers. In this case, you should use the Vertical Circular Movement exercise (see Chapter 2), alternately using your left and right hands to direct the sound. Make sure that you end the siren sound *before* you finish pulling in your hand toward the center of vital energy. It is important to continue to pull in the sound, even after you end it. This will help your abdominal muscles remain firm so that your breath energy (ch'i) will not slacken. The sound should always end with firm breath energy behind it.

An extension of the Siren Sound exercise is to reverse the direction and go from your low register to your high register, eventually connecting the two directions in continuous circles. This variation is especially good in helping you to sing or to speak high notes with a free, rich, and resonant voice.

Delightfully Surprised

Imagine that you are delightfully surprised, as if you are meeting an old friend you haven't seen in a long time. This feeling of surprise will express itself in different ways. For a lot of people, it causes their mouths to drop open and the space at the back of the mouth to open wider. Now gently exclaim, "ah!" in a medium-high or high falsetto pitch. This will quickly give you an open throat, if it is not already so. In order to become aware of this openness in the upper throat, hold the "ah" for a couple of seconds.

Imagined Inhaling

To keep an open throat while you are singing, you should imagine, as you are producing the sound, that you are inhaling air through the center of spirit, down toward the center of vital energy. Although you are of course not actually inhaling while singing, using your imagination in this way is a psychophysical technique based on Taoist spiritual approaches and will help you achieve marked results in voice production. In this case, imagining that you are bringing air in through the region between and behind your eyebrows, and not your nose and mouth, will open up more space at the back of your mouth, help prevent your throat from closing up, and give you more resonance. Here is another case where you can apply the Vertical Circular Movement exercise described in Chapter 2.

Imagined Gargling

Another way of getting an open throat is to imagine that you are gargling on a round "ah" sound. Focus your attention on gargling at the upper throat, just behind the roof of the mouth. Try it first with about half a teaspoon of water, putting your head back so the water rests in the back of your mouth. As you gargle, feel the stretching and opening of the upper throat. Swallow the water, then do the imagined gargling with your head in a normal upright position, re-creating that open-throat feeling. When you sing, you stretch the upper throat in a similar way, varying it according to need.

After experimenting with all five of these exercises, use the ones that suit you best. Practicing them will help you become aware of achieving a good, open throat. Gradually you will form the habit of opening your throat when you sing or speak, without thinking about any of the exercises. Daily practice, even for ten minutes, will help you develop the good habits of maintaining a flexible, open throat, producing a resonant, full-range voice with varied dynamics.

Maintaining an Adequate Space in the Mouth Opening

Although it is important for you to have an open throat when singing, you must also have an adequate space in the mouth opening. To make sure you are allowing adequate space, put your index and middle fingers together and insert them between your teeth, as shown in Figure 38. Vocalize on the vowels "oo," "aw," and "ah" with an open throat, using the Vertical Circular Movement exercise from Chapter 2. After a couple of minutes, take the fingers away and vocalize without them.

Vocalize with the fingers in as well as out of your mouth several times. At first you may feel that your jaw is a little sore or uncomfortable. Don't worry; this feeling will be gone rather quickly. Very soon you will form the habit of maintaining an adequate mouth opening for proper voice production.

FIGURE 38

In principle, high and loud notes require a larger space; soft notes and low and middle-range notes need a smaller space. Through constant practice and use of your voice, you will learn to adjust the space accordingly. The mouth opening will also vary with different vowel and consonant sounds. For instance, you will find that the space for the vowel "ah" is not the same as for the vowel "oo" or "ee." The space for the consonant "s" is not the same as for the consonant "v." Also, because it is hard to keep the mouth and throat open while lingering on a consonant, it is important to finish pronouncing consonants as quickly as possible.

While doing this exercise, adjust the position of your hand, wrist, and fingers to be as comfortable as possible. Don't tighten your mouth or lips or use your neck muscles to pull your lower lip and chin down. Let your relaxed lower lip barely cover your lower teeth, as this will help prevent tightening in your throat. Remember, as in all the exercises, to use both hands alternately.

Producing Good Tones by Proper Inhaling

Some singers inhale through their noses and only open their mouths when they start to sing. While it is true that the air inhaled through your nose is cleaner, it is faster, easier, and more effective if you inhale through your nose and open throat with your mouth open. This really won't hurt your health; the fact is that every day of your life, in talking to people, you have been inhaling with your mouth open. Some people also breathe through their mouths when they sleep.

When you sing your voice is required to do much more than when you speak, including sustaining long notes and producing a wider vocal range, richer resonance, greater variety of dynamics, and a great variation of pitch. Timing is also much more important. You will sing better and breathe more quickly if you remember to inhale through all three passages—your nose, mouth, and open throat. If you do this on an imagined round "ah" sound, the back of your throat will open to form the largest space possible, helping you to produce a free and resonant sound. Once your throat is opened, you will be able to sing on any vowel.

As with all breathing discussed in this book, remember to imagine the air following a path of continuous circular movement. Then, when you actually start to sing, imagine that the sound is following the same path. After you practice this for a period of time, you will feel as if sound flows into you from your breath, and the breath flows into you from the sound. You will feel a smooth transition from breath to sound, and from sound to breath. You will breathe more deeply and more quickly and will need less breath to sing with. Rather than producing harsh sounds, you will simply feel that your voice is free and flows with resonance. (This approach will also help you prepare to give a speech or dramatic reading without a microphone in a big hall.)

So, welcome the sound into your being by opening your heart and inhaling through your center of spirit, your nose, your mouth, and your open throat.

Taking a Double Breath for Long Notes and Phrases

Sometimes, if you need a little more breath to sustain a long note or phrase, you should take what I call a "double breath." That is, as soon as you have actually inhaled and directed the breath to the center of vital energy, and you feel that that area is slightly firm and the lower back is slightly expanded, take a quick additional breath, right away directing it to the back of your waist. You will notice your lower back and waistline expand slightly more and the center of your lower abdomen will feel a bit firmer. Make sure you don't take too much breath. Take as much as you need, as long as your body does not become rigid. You should still feel flexibility throughout your body and throat. This technique will enable you to do sustained singing with ease.

Pointers and Exercises for Extending Your Vocal Range

When we speak of vocal range, we mean the range of notes a singer's voice encompasses, from the very lowest to the highest. Without a doubt it is important to develop a good middle range before spending time and energy trying to get high and low notes. However, it does not mean that you should not try to sing your high and low notes, even as you are developing a free, flexible middle range, as long as you don't hurt your throat. Use the following exercises, but do not spend too much time on them before your middle range is in good form.

High Notes

Cultivate the habit of not taking in too much breath before you sing high notes. You shouldn't need much more breath when singing high notes than when singing middle-range notes. Take in as much as you can, as long as your body doesn't feel rigid. You should feel that the center of vital energy is getting slightly firm.

Many people have a tendency to force out a great deal of breath in order to get out their high notes. You should never do this. First of all, it isn't necessary, because only the front tip of the vocal cords is used to produce high notes. This area is small and light, so it doesn't need a lot of air to move it and produce the tone. Second, forcing the breath up and out will produce tension in the throat, overloading the delicate vocal cords. Instead, just imagine that you keep your ch'i (breath energy) flowing.

Before working on high notes, review for a few minutes the exercises described earlier on producing good tones by proper inhaling and on opening the throat. The best open-throat exercises to use here are Siren Sound and

About to Yawn. When practicing Siren Sound, do it for a couple of minutes and sing as high as you can without straining your throat. Open your throat more on the high notes and less on the middle and lower notes. Keep in mind the image of the sound following the path of continuous circular movement. Use hand movements to direct the sound, if needed. When creating the siren sound, you should feel that you are welcoming the sound with enthusiasm and energy. The intensity will tend to be a bit lower as you go down to your lower range, but don't let it sag.

Singing high notes is similar in many ways to singing mid-range notes. For example, just before you actually sing a high note, try to *hear* the tone you would like to produce. Imagine that you are pulling in the sound. Don't try to push the note out. The popular notion of "hitting" a high note really doesn't work. This is because the thought of "hitting" a note immediately makes you want to push a lot of air out, which will tighten your throat. Also, when you use too much air pressure, you strain your vocal cords and your voice does not sound free.

Sing the beginning of your high notes with confidence, enthusiasm, and precision and without fear or hesitation. Open your mouth and throat to their widest comfortable positions and drop your jaw, but not so far that you cause strain. Get the consonants out of the way as quickly as you can.

When you sing a high note, sing the preceding note slightly softer. This will help you sing your high notes with much more ease. While you are singing a long high note, make sure your jaw is not locked. You should have a feeling of flexibility.

A very good sound to start with when practicing your high notes is the round "ah" vowel. Another good one is the French vowel "en." You can try adding initial consonants as well, if you like. Other possibilities include "aw," "oh," "oo," "er" (as in "bird"), "mah," "hah," "haw," "sah," "fah," "faw," "soo," "sen" (as in French "en"), and "may."

While inhaling or singing, imagine that all the vowels you sing are round and that your upper throat is arched and round, like an inverted "U" shape. Your throat should have a feeling of openness.

Keep in mind that rhythm is the pulse of music, its life force. You can use it to help you sing the high notes. By paying attention to rhythm in your singing, you will avoid hesitation or letting your energy drag. You can think of this as being like the flying of a kite, which I described in the beginning of Chapter 2. The stronger beats in the music are like the stronger gusts of wind blowing on the kite, while the weaker beats are like a lessening of the wind.

Using rhythm, you will vary the sound you produce, just as the kite flyer varies the strength or gentleness with which the string is pulled, depending on the wind and the desired effects. Rhythm thus can lead you naturally into using the interplay of opposite forces (dynamics, in this case), and the pulsations of the music can help you to unblock your inhibitions.

Practice your high notes using the Vertical Circular Movement exercise discussed in Chapter 2. Using your full voice on the strong beat of the rhythm, pull in the note on the downward movement of the circle. Using your softer voice, let the weak beat carry the note through the upward movement of the circle. You can also practice using one turn of the circle for individual notes, singing each one with a crescendo and a decrescendo. Use a moderate tempo first, as a slow tempo may cause you to lose momentum. Establish a steady rhythm before you sing your high notes, and remember to end each note by pulling it into you.

Cultivate the good habit of singing high notes without fear. When you sing in your medium and medium-high ranges, you usually have a sense of confidence and ease. When singing high notes, try to remember this feeling of confidence and ease. When you sing your high notes with ease, you will become more confident of your voice, so you will sing better and will be able to express the emotion of the song with spontaneity.

Following are specific exercises to use when practicing high notes.

Rising to Receive Your Full Voice

Sit on the edge of a chair, leaning slightly forward, with both feet on the floor. The feet should be a few inches apart, one in front of the other. The front foot is fully relaxed on the floor while the back foot rests on the toes.

Begin singing a tone and, shifting the weight to the front foot, slowly rise from the chair. The toes of the back foot help to move the body weight forward and up. Start with a tone in the middle of your vocal range; you can move into higher and lower tones from this place. Remember not to strain your voice!

As you rise, keep opening your upper throat and imagine that your voice is like a sunbeam moving through your center of spirit and down through your center of vital energy, continuing downward deep into the earth. Your voice will sound fuller if your can feel yourself grounded to earth and your voice connected to your center of vital energy.

If your voice is still not feeling full and resonant, add the following hand movement to the exercise: Raise one hand as you inhale. As soon as your hand is above your forehead, start singing a tone while pulling the hand slowly down toward the center of vital energy. Imagine that the sound moves downward with your hand motion. As soon as the hand reaches the navel area, stop singing and, keeping the mouth open, pull downward for another second.

Waltzing

Practice your high notes while dancing a waltz or simply turning in a circle. Waltzing and turning are forms of continuous circular movement that are used in many places around the world to unblock inhibitions and fear. I prefer the waltz because it combines the use of rhythm. Practice just the waltzing first, until you feel comfortable and free in the movement. Then begin to sing, taking your high note at the start of a turn—that moment when the weight of your body is on the ball of your foot. Then hold your high note without straining while you continue to waltz. You'll be amazed at how easily your sound will flow out! While the notes may not sound sturdy given the continuous movement of the body, this exercise will help you to experience the high note and feel its sensation in your head and body.

Walking Backward

Practice your high notes while walking backward. Start your high note just as the foot you are stepping backward onto touches the ground. There is a wonderful feeling of "grounding" the note in this exercise. As you step backward, lean forward gently with slightly bent knees.

Standing on One Leg

This exercise involves practicing your high notes while standing on one leg and bending that knee, letting your body sink. Take the high note as you begin to bend the knee; sustain the note as you continue to bend. Bend your knees only to the point where it is still easy to get up. As in the Waltzing exercise, practice the movement before actually singing.

Bending the knee on one leg helps to center the energy in the Tan-T'ien area. While bending the knee, imagine that you are pulling in the sound with one hand, or simply imagine that the sound comes into you from heaven through your center of spirit and then into your Tan-T'ien, then travels down to the center of the earth.

Embracing

Practice high notes while embracing someone with enthusiasm. If there's not another person around, embrace a pillow. Make sure your whole body, especially the center of vital energy, is involved. If you don't have someone to embrace physically, pretend that you do. Imagine that you take in the high note (or that it flows into you) quickly, without hesitation, right at the moment you start the embrace. Embracing with enthusiasm helps to activate the whole being, enabling you to reach higher notes and enriching the resonance of your voice.

Emptying the Breath

In Taoist meditation, as in Buddhist meditation, to empty the mind is to clear it and to free it from tension so that it can be fresh when it is used again. In singing, emptying the breath is one of the best ways to reach the high notes more easily and to gain more resonance. Bend your body very slightly forward, as if you are about to bow, while exhaling all the breath you have, so your lower abdomen is completely sucked in. As soon as you feel that you have emptied all your breath, straighten up again while taking in an easy and smooth breath on an imagined round "ah" sound. (Be sure not to inhale too much, as it will make your body rigid.) Your breath will quickly go deep into the center of vital energy. You then sing your note while imagining you are pulling in the sound.

Do this exercise five or six times in succession, but not for a prolonged period of time. It will give you a good sense of breathing deeply to activate the energy flow to the center of vital energy, and you will not feel that your high notes are as high as they were before. They will come more easily, and your sound will be fuller.

LOW NOTES

There are several effective ways to extend your low vocal range. One of the best is to focus on the flow of continuous circular movement while practicing your low notes. This will give you a feeling of flexibility, which is just as important when singing low notes as when singing notes in the high or middle ranges.

Don't let your energy sag while singing your low notes. Sing them with a feeling of welcome and admiration, as expressed in the sound "ah." Try singing them as if you are about to speak, using a small mouth opening and keeping a slightly open throat. Never push your low notes out. Also, don't press your jaw or chin down, or your low notes will not sound as though they are freely produced. Not only that, but you will be putting undue pressure on your vocal cords, which will harm them.

If you go from a low note to a high note, or even to a note half a tone higher, and you want a smooth transition between the two notes, sing the ending of the lower note slightly more softly, before going to the higher note. Sing the beginning of the high note almost as softly as the ending of the preceding low note. In cases where the high note is meant to be loud, make the transition as quickly as possible, thus getting to the loud sound without delay.

Practice your low notes at first using a moderate or moderately slow tempo. Then sing them however you like.

Exercises for Extending Your Dynamics

When we speak of dynamics in music, we are referring to the degree of loudness and softness. Variations of dynamics enhance the emotion and meaning of a song, just as variations in rhythm, tempo, and tonal color do. In Taoist terms, such variations signify the interplay of polarities or contrasting elements.

TABLE 1
TERMINOLOGY FOR DYNAMICS IN MUSIC

Italian term	Musical abbreviation	English equivalent
Fortissimo	*ff*	Very loud
Forte	*f*	Loud
Mezzo forte	*mf*	Moderately loud
Mezzo piano	*mp*	Moderately soft
Piano	*p*	Soft
Pianissimo	*pp*	Very soft

The terms that are commonly used to describe degrees of loudness in music are given in Table 1. Some composers go beyond even this range in making sure that their composition will be played with great dynamic contrast. For instance, Tchaikovsky marked "*ppppp*" at the end of the first movement of his sixth symphony, while Verdi in his opera "Aida" indicated "*ppp*" at the end of the tenor aria "Celeste Aida."

Singers who observe the general range of dynamics faithfully are considered to have a wide range, enabling them to interpret songs expressively. Since each voice has its own character and is different from every other voice, it should be noted that the dynamic levels will vary slightly according to the individual voice. In other words, my soft voice is not exactly the same in degree of softness as your soft voice; the same is true for our loud voices.

The following pointers and exercises will help you to extend your dynamic range to its fullest and maintain a good range, once you have achieve it.

SINGING *PIANISSIMO*

Practice the Siren Sound exercise described earlier in this chapter. Do it smoothly and gently with an open throat and a feeling of flexibility in your throat and jaw. Your body should also be free from tension.

As always, even when singing softly, keep your energy high; don't let it sag.

For soft tones, your mouth opening should be smaller than it is for loud tones, and it should be as close to a round shape as possible. Let your lower lip relax, barely covering your lower teeth.

Take deep breaths smoothly, gently, and without effort, making sure that you take in only a small amount of breath. You will find that it is easier to sing soft notes using less breath.

When you start to sing a very soft note, imagine you are taking the note in gently, quickly, and with confidence. Simultaneously, you should open your throat and mouth just a bit more. Remember the exercises for continuous circular movement. Here, you should imagine that you are inhaling the very soft note—that the *pianissimo* sound is like a cloud floating through you.

Vocalize on the round "ah," "oh," and "oo" vowels. Imagine that your tone is round and has a soft, ringing quality. Continue vocalizing, using the "ee" and "ay" (as in "bay") vowels. Choose the vowel sounds with which you feel most comfortable. Some singers feel that "ee" and "ay" are the most helpful when singing very soft notes, while others prefer "ah," "oh," and "oo."

Next vocalize by adding consonants such as "m," "w," "f," and "v" to the vowel sounds, making sounds such as "mah" and "we." When you vocalize with any consonant preceding the vowel, you should leave the consonant as quickly as possible. If you find that adding the consonants before the vowels is not helpful at first, then wait a while before trying them again.

If you feel you are not energized and focused before you vocalize, or if you feel your breath is not going down easily to the Tan-T'ien area, first do a few minutes of the Grand Solar Circle, Flapping My Wings, and Moving Meditation exercises in Chapter 3. These will boost your energy without strain and will help you to coordinate your breath and energy for proper tonal production.

It is also important for you to learn to make shifts in dynamics smoothly and effectively, such as when a very soft note is preceded by a loud note. Sing the ending of the loud note softly, gradually but quickly decreasing the volume of the loud note before coming to the very soft note. If the composer does not want this, the soft note will be marked "*subito p*" (suddenly *pianissimo*). Another such shift, singing from a very soft dynamic and gradually going to a very loud sound and then back to very soft (crescendo to decrescendo), can best be achieved by using the Vertical Circular Movement exercise given in Chapter 2. As the circle comes down and in toward you, gradually increase your volume. When the circle is going up and out, decrease your volume. You should feel as if you are gently and steadily pulling in the note as the sound comes to an end.

SINGING *FORTISSIMO*

Singers who are healthy, energetic, and full of vitality will find it easier to sing *fortissimo* than those with less strength. However, singing *fortissimo* does not mean that you need to use a lot of force or breath to push your sound out. Some people take in too much breath, which makes the body and throat become rigid, producing a tone that sounds strained and is not as rich or loud as it could be. As a rule, you can take in as much breath as you like, so long as you remain flexible throughout your body and throat. Direct your breath deep into your center of vital energy, causing that area to become firm.

Don't push the sound out, and don't think of hitting the note with all your might. If you do, you will tighten your throat, and the sound will not come out well. You shouldn't even think of projecting your sound out too far. Instead, using the open-throat exercises described earlier in this chapter, simply imagine you are pulling in the sound with great enthusiasm and confidence and without hesitation. Make sure that the beginning of the sound is slightly soft but flows very quickly into *forte* or *fortissimo*.

To sing *fortissimo*, your throat and body have to be free from tension. You should maintain a healthy balance between relaxation and excitation, not only when singing a very loud note, but also before singing it. The Vertical Circular Movement exercise described in Chapter 2 is a great help in maintaining such a balance and makes it easier to sing *fortissimo*. As you allow your breath and sound to flow through you, open your heart and your whole being to receive the wonderful sonic vibration of the great universe, which is joining its power with you at that particular moment.

Another good way to use your imagination when singing a loud or very loud long note, also as discussed in Chapter 2, is to imagine that your sound is traveling very fast, toward the center of the Earth. To increase the loudness gradually, simply imagine that your sound goes increasingly faster. A variation on this is to imagine that your sound, in the form of a radiant sunbeam, is chasing a ball very fast, down toward the center of the Earth. If you want to increase the loudness, imagine that your sound chases after the ball faster and faster.

Several of the exercises for singing high notes, described earlier in the chapter, will also help you to sing *fortissimo*. Two in particular are Standing on One Leg and Embracing. A variation of Embracing can be used when you sing a string of loud and moderately loud notes in moderate or slow tempo. Firmly embrace a person on the loud note and release the embrace slightly on the moderately loud note. This is another way of applying the interplay of opposite forces. Instead of pushing out a great deal of breath to produce a loud sound, you pull in or embrace firmly to produce a loud sound. It is important to remember that you should also start and end the phrase by pulling in or embracing the sound, even though you intend to sing it loudly. Of course, it would be the unaccented syllables and unimportant words that you would sing less loudly. You can do the embracing exercise in your imagination (kinesthetically), or you might even try it with a pillow. It works very well.

When you practice singing *fortissimo*, you should make your fullest sound, singing close to your maximum volume. Bear in mind, however, that to a listener a very loud note will not sound very loud if *all* the notes you sing are loud. The perception of loudness and softness is a matter of contrast. So, if you want to sound very loud, you should sing the preceding notes more softly.

A very loud note usually expresses the climax of an emotional build-up in a song. Singers tend to respond to this build-up by becoming tense themselves, before reaching the very loud note. This is a trap, because nobody can sing well under tension. Remind yourself to breathe smoothly and deeply between phrases, as often as the music permits; to keep a flexible and open throat; to relax your jaw, mouth, and body; and to bend your knees slightly. If you do, you will be able to sing *fortissimo* with ease.

At the same time, it helps if you have one foot slightly in front of the other, allowing the weight of your body to lean slightly forward. Remain relaxed and steady, and avoid shifting your body weight back and forth over your feet. Let your upper body rest comfortably over your hips.

Finally, you will find that the vowel "ah" carries high loud notes very well and so is particularly good for vocalizing. Avoid singing vowels that strain your throat or do not show off the good qualities of your voice.

Knowing When Your Tone Is Good

When developing your voice you will progress faster if you know what kind of sound you want to produce. A clear, correct tonal image in your mind's ear is essential and will determine the quality of the sound you will sing. Remember that whether the tone is *beautiful* or not is very much a matter of personal taste. What you are aiming for at this point is to develop your awareness of *good* tone, which is a more objective judgment made by applying certain standards. The following suggestions will help you to judge when your tonal image is correct and when your resulting tone is good.

First, listen to fine singers in person or on recordings. If possible, listen to the best singers, and listen to them often, so you will form a clear concept of good tones by which to guide yourself.

It is also very important to take lessons with a good teacher, preferably the best you can find and someone you like. The teacher can clarify your concept of good tones and tell you which of your tones are good and which are harsh or unpleasant. She or he can also show you how to produce your tone correctly, leading you to the right path for developing your singing potential.

Record your voice when you practice, and listen to the playback. Good, high-fidelity recording and playback equipment is essential, otherwise the recorded sound will be distorted. Listening on your own and with your teacher will help you to clarify your judgments about the quality of the tone you produce. It is important to understand that, if you have not heard your voice recorded, you will have difficulty knowing what your voice truly sounds like.

This is because the sound you hear in your inner ear when you sing, the sound others hear when you sing, and the sound you hear on a recording of your voice are all different. It takes time to recognize which one is your true voice. After you hear your own recorded voice often, you can gradually recognize your voice and its various shades and colors. Before the invention of the tape recorder, it was the singers' teachers and colleagues who helped them to form their concept of their own tonal image.

Your judgment of good tones is based on your ability to recognize certain vocal qualities, and on your feeling of physical flexibility while singing or speaking. Qualities that you should recognize include

- A clear and smooth tone with an even vibrato (not a tremolo or shaking sound).
- A ringing quality in your voice. (Strong and rich tone has a more intense ringing quality, while very soft tone has a delicate ringing quality.)
- The ability to sing your notes on pitch, consistently.
- A roundness in the formation of vowel sounds.

Listening frequently and critically to good and bad tones, sung not only by yourself but by others, will help you form the clear tonal image that you need to guide you when you sing.

While you are singing you will also learn to recognize the physical sensation of singing with both good and bad tones. When you sing and produce good tones, you should feel

- No tension in the throat
- Openness and flexibility, especially at the back of the mouth and the upper throat
- Flexibility and freedom when singing loudly or softly, quickly or slowly, high or low, and when creating the various shades of vocal color, such as bright and somber

If, on the other hand, you feel tension and tightness in your throat and if you strain when singing in your vocal range, you will know the tones are not correctly produced.

In addition to recognizing tonal qualities and certain physical sensations, you can also imagine round tones coming to you in various forms, such as a radiant sun, a bright full moon, or splendid blossoms. Use any image you find helpful.

If you begin to notice a tone that you think is beautiful, recognize and remember it. If other people think that your tone is merely good, but not beautiful, don't feel badly about it. As the saying goes, "Beauty is in the eyes of the beholder."

Learning to Carry a Tune

If your hearing is good, if your voice is healthy, and if you speak with a normal range of inflection and pitch, not in a monotone, you will have a very good chance of learning to carry a tune. You will learn to sing well if you have a strong desire to learn and the faith that you will succeed. Good results come with proper instruction and constant practice, done with a "smiling heart."

What is meant by "carrying a tune" is the ability to remember a melody formed by a series of notes, and to sing that melody accurately on pitch, when singing alone or with others. The following are some of the reasons that people come to believe that they can't learn to carry a tune.

1. When they were children they were asked not to sing or were simply told to "shut up," which caused a significant mental block.
2. They seldom sing, by themselves or with others; hence they rarely get any practice. Their voices are unused to producing musical sounds, and their minds are not used to remembering tunes.
3. Although they think they are listening to a tune they want to learn, they can't focus their attention on what they are hearing, so they don't learn the tune well enough to sing it correctly.
4. Whenever they start to sing, their fear or their inability to use their voice well causes their throat to tighten, their voice to shake, and their range to become limited to perhaps five or six notes.
5. They become so nervous whenever they start to sing that they cannot clearly hear the tune they are trying to sing or even what they are singing.

I have used the approaches discussed in this section to help people learn to carry a tune. I also find it helpful to remind my students that the knowledge and ability to carry a tune are already encoded in them, so what they really are doing is decoding that knowledge and ability. They are taking action to *remind* themselves what to do—how to carry a tune. This idea will be discussed in more detail in Chapter 6, in the discussion on memorizing music.

The following pointers and exercises are designed to solve the specific vocal problem of difficulty in carrying a tune. Try them all, to see which are most helpful. In the beginning, when your self-evaluation may not be keen enough, someone with a good ear for singing (your teacher or a friend) can help you evaluate yourself.

First, stand with good posture and do the Siren Sound exercise described in the beginning of the chapter. Sing within your vocal range, starting as high as you can without straining your voice. This exercise will give you an open throat, which is essential for free and rich tonal production, a wide vocal range, and a variety of dynamics. After you practice it for a short period of time, you will be able to produce tones with better resonance and you will have a wider vocal range. These good and free sonic vibrations in you will increase your confidence in yourself and help you sense the pitch of your voice.

Get a teacher or friend with a good ear to guide you into hearing what your best vocal range is at the moment. Start to vocalize within that vocal range. Do the vocal exercises in Chapter 4, first using Exercise 1, which is a five-note exercise, and then Exercise 2, which uses the same five notes, but going both up and down. Don't try to change keys until you can carry the "tune" of the exercise in one key first. After vocalizing using Exercise 1, you can add more notes at the top or bottom, but stay in one key.

If you know how to play the piano or organ, it will help a lot. Play Exercises 1 and 2 on a keyboard first; listen to them without tension. (Make sure the instrument is in tune.) Keep vocalizing, using one exercise at first, followed after a few minutes by the other. Sometimes it will help you catch the tune faster if someone sings along with you at first, or sings the exercise for you. You should then repeat what you have heard.

Usually people learn to carry a tune by listening to a human voice rather than an instrument. In general, it doesn't make any difference whether you listen to a voice of the same or opposite sex, although some people feel they catch on faster when listening to a voice of the same sex.

When you think you have the tune right, record it and play it back. Check with your teacher or friend to find out whether or not you are singing correctly. Try to judge for yourself whether you are carrying the tune or not. If you record yourself while singing incorrectly, you will sharpen your sense—through hearing your mistakes—of what is wrong and what is right. Record your subsequent attempts to carry the tune correctly, and play them back. When you hear yourself singing the right way, your self-evaluation will be sharpened and your confidence will increase. This will strengthen your ability to carry a tune.

As you can see, a major part of this process is learning to listen, but don't listen too hard. Use the Taoist approach. Let the tune or phrase flow into you. Practice with enthusiasm, and never let yourself become bored, as you will never achieve good results when in this state.

Practice when you are alert, and choose comfortable surroundings. Tiredness and overheated or very cold rooms are not conducive to effective practice. Choose simple songs within your vocal range and practice them at a comfortable, moderate tempo, even if that is not how they are written. After you have learned to carry the tune well, you can go to the original tempo. Nursery rhymes and folk songs are often good choices, as they don't require a big vocal range and their rhythms are usually easy to learn. You can also pick up some phrases from a particular song you like, and practice only those phrases if the other parts of the song are not suitable for your vocal range.

You don't have to love everything you sing, but you should never sing anything you dislike.

If you have a strong desire to sing along with a record, let your teacher or friend help you choose the record suitable for you.

If you practice faithfully and regularly, you will have a very good chance of learning to carry a tune. In the meantime, as your voice gets better, you'll enjoy singing more, and this will keep your motivation high.

Curing Off-Pitch Singing

Singing off pitch means that you are singing just a little too high or too low for the written pitch—a little sharp or a little flat. Off-pitch singing is annoying and can ruin the sound of music. It may be caused by various technical, physical, mental, or emotional factors, singly or in combination. The following approaches will help you to correct this problem.

To begin with, it is important that you open your heart, be alert and energetic, and keep your attention focused. If you are tired or if your voice is tired, get a good rest before singing. Relax yourself by doing the body movement exercises. Try to breathe smoothly and deeply, with a feeling of flexibility in your throat and throughout your body. Keep your energy flowing.

Inhale smoothly and deeply through a flexible, open throat, directing the breath through the center of spirit and vital energy. Inhale on an imagined round "ah" sound (see earlier section of this chapter, on "Producing Good Tones by Proper Inhaling").

Choose a song that you like, one that is within your comfortable vocal range. Before you start to sing, try to "hear" clearly in your mind's ear the specific interval, or whole musical phrase you have learned. You should do this without constantly going to the piano or listening to a tape. This approach will help strengthen your memory of the music and will improve your ability to sing on pitch. Be sure, however, to adopt the Taoist concept of doing nothing in excess. Don't listen too hard. Listen to the song and sing it like a child without any inhibitions. Allow the sound to flow into you.

If you have a problem singing on pitch on a specific note, have someone sing or play the note on the piano while you turn your whole body around several times. You should do this while imagining that the pitch and sound are flowing into you. Then sing the note. This is another way of applying the Taoist concept of continuous circular movement to unblock your energy channels and release your inhibitions, allowing you to sing on the correct pitch.

Don't "hit" the note, as too much initial force can distort your pitch. Sing softer on the first moment of the note, whether or not the note is meant to be sung softly. Sing it while imagining that you are pulling it in at a high speed, bringing the sound in through the center of spirit, down toward the center of vital energy and deep into the earth. Imagining pulling in the sound at high speed produces high energy for your voice. This will generally help you to sing on pitch, but it is especially good with problems on high notes. (For low notes, remember that, although they do not require high energy, you must not let your energy sag, or you may go flat.) This technique also works well when you practice sustaining a long note. You can also imagine the sound traveling in a smooth, continuous circular movement. When you have a tremolo or wobble, which is another form of off-pitch singing, use this technique while imagining that the sound flows into you like a smooth, straight, radiant sunbeam.

While staying on the same pitch, sing a series of words having both consonants and vowels (e.g., "My life and love"). Sing the consonants as quickly as you can. Keep your attention focused and your energy flowing all the time, especially when you are singing a series of notes on the same pitch, as repetition can cause a singer to become careless or too relaxed and to sing flat.

If there are notes occurring often in a song in the weak areas of your voice—usually in the extreme high or lower register or in the area where the "break" in your voice occurs—change the key to something more suitable. It is harder for you to correct off-pitch singing in those weak and vulnerable areas. Your chances of solving the problem even in these areas are very good if, in addition to doing the exercises just mentioned, you also do the open-throat exercises described at the beginning of this chapter. While vocalizing on notes in the "voice break" area, practice first with an "oo" sound, as in "too." Then continue to hold your lips as if pronouncing "oo," but sing "ee," as in "see." Remember to pull in the sound.

While you are singing, imagine that your voice is a radiant and sturdy sunbeam flowing smoothly and steadily in and out of your being. Imagine that the sound of your voice is vibrant and brilliant, like sunlight, especially when you have a tendency to sing flat.

Take good care of your health. Your voice will wobble if you are feeling weak or low (see Chapter 8).

Finally, one of the common causes of a tremolo or wobble, or of singing off pitch, is stage fright. The section in Chapter 6 on "Transforming Stage Fright into Stage Joy" can be of great help in this regard.

6

Techniques for Performers and Advanced Students

The purpose of learning is to put into use what you have learned.

CHINESE AXIOM

It is a joy to make your favorite songs a part of you. A song does not really become a part of you until you incorporate it into your memory. This chapter will introduce effective ways to memorize a song, leaving all of your energies available to sing with freedom and feeling.

Giving Your Spirit Flight: Singing from Memory

Sometimes tradition permits you to look at a vocal score, as when you are performing oratorios or singing in church services. Usually, however, you are expected to sing from memory, and this is most definitely true in operatic or theatrical productions. Even when you can look at the vocal score while singing, to do so will divert at least some of your energy and attention from interpreting the song to looking at the words and music. It will also interfere with the spontaneous flow of your voice and feelings. Sometimes a very experienced artist may be able to take occasional quick glances at the score and still keep in close contact with the music and the audience. No song, however, can be sung expressively to an audience if the singer's eyes are focused on the vocal score.

There is broad support for this position among many of the best vocal teachers and experts, both contemporary and historical. For example, Carlo Lamperti, in his 1954 book entitled *Improving Your Voice*, notes that "even an experienced singer will use more breath in learning a new song than in singing one already known" (p. 23).[1] My own singing teacher at Columbia University Teachers College, Professor Harry R. Wilson, often urged me and my fellow students to sing from memory, and I noticed that we did in fact sing much better when we had memorized the songs. Our voices sounded better and we projected more emotions. When I studied with Alexander Kipnis, I got more out of his interpretation when he demonstrated the song to me from memory. There was a sense of immediacy then, in his emotional response to the song. Although he was in his eighties and his voice did not have the splendor of his younger days, his eyes, face, body movements, and hand gestures expressed his feelings about the song.

My experience with my own students has also borne this out. When they have memorized a song, I can help them improve their voice production and interpretation much more quickly than if they have to use a score.

If you have difficulty in memorizing songs, the approaches discussed in this section can help you.

CREATING HARMONIOUS CONDITIONS FOR MEMORIZING

It is important to give serious attention to attitudes and actions that will make memorization easy and enjoyable. You need to find ways to sustain your enthusiasm for singing and your interest in sharing this joy with other people.

Choose a time when you are physically and mentally alert. If you are sleepy, very tired, or feeling irritated or uncomfortable, don't try to memorize; you will achieve little. If you are mentally tired, give your mind a chance to rest for awhile, by walking or doing nonstrenuous exercises, including the body movement exercises mentioned in Chapter 3. After a good rest, your mind will be refreshed.

If your mind needs a deeper rest, it will be good for you to meditate deeply, emptying your mind temporarily. This is a Buddhist as well as a Taoist practice that revitalizes the mind and elevates the spirit. To get to such a deep meditative state, you will need to discipline yourself to practice meditation regularly. A master's guidance will be helpful.

To motivate yourself to get started, set a goal for memorizing one song. For instance, schedule yourself to sing two weeks from now at a party, in a class, in a concert, on TV, or simply for someone special. Your goal can be for a real or an imagined event, but of course it is better if the event is real. When you have a purpose for memorizing a song, you will most likely get the work done faster. The more clear, definite, and absorbing the goal is, the more quickly you will reach it. There must be more than just an enthusiastic urge and a desire to learn; there must be a burning desire to learn by a definite time and for an interesting purpose.

Select songs that appeal to you, suit your style and your voice, and are relatively short (a good length is about two or three minutes). They should not be too complex in rhythm or language or too fast in tempo. Once you have memorized some songs, learned certain skills of memorizing, and gained confidence in your ability to remember, it will be easier for you to memorize longer, faster, and more complex songs. The first song is the hardest, but with practice each one becomes easier. We learn by doing, and so we learn to memorize by memorizing.

When memorizing, work in a quiet and well-ventilated place with a comfortable temperature. You will memorize better if you practice in several short periods rather than in one long period. Memorizing just before going to bed can also be very effective, as it will facilitate subconscious learning.

Professor Mary Schmitt, a neurophysiologist who has taught at the New School for Social Research in New York City, has made some interesting observations about learning, which she has shared with me, and which may shed some light on the nature of subconscious learning. She claims, "We carry within us two billion years of evolution, two billion years of memory. Much of what we call 'learning' is no more than remembering, or bringing to consciousness what we already know."[2] Inspired by this idea, I have passed it along to my students, telling them, "What you are learning now is nothing new; you have only forgotten what you already know. I am here to remind you to remember." My students have told me that this thought has given them more confidence in themselves, making them feel they can learn faster and memorize better.

APPROACHES TO MEMORIZING MUSIC

There has been considerable research conducted over the past decades into the functioning of the brain and how people learn. Some of these findings are good to bear in mind when approaching the memorization of music. In particular, according to research conducted in the late 1970s by neurologists Antonio and

Hanna Damasio, there is evidence that the verbal processing that enables a singer to sing the words of a song is very different from the processing necessary for uttering the same words outside a musical or poetic context. The Damasios' work is summarized as follows in a 1979 *New York Times* article:[3]

> These researchers think that "the verbal language used in song is probably generated by right hemisphere function and is therefore close to the origin of the melody itself." There is no hemispheric conflict because the right hemisphere remains in charge and directs traffic. . . . To oversimply, language skills and analytical abilities are centered in the left hemisphere while emotion and intuition are the province of the right. About 25 years ago, it was discovered that "the right hemisphere is overwhelmingly concerned with musical ability." Many studies since then have re-endorsed that finding.

The article further quotes the Damasios as proposing that "language and music unite in the right hemisphere in order to escape interhemispheric rivalry".

The most obvious implication that such findings have for learning to sing songs by heart is the importance of practicing both the music and lyrics together, at least some of the time, so the two do not become isolated from each other in different hemispheres of the brain.

It is important to begin with songs that will be easiest for you. To that end, memorize songs in your native tongue first, or in a foreign language you know well. After you have increased your confidence in your ability to memorize, you can learn songs in languages you don't know well, or learn longer or more complex pieces.

Get good recordings of the songs you are going to memorize, preferably in the key in which you are going to sing them. If possible get a recording sung by a great artist. Listen to it and follow along with the vocal score. Get good recordings of the piano accompaniments of your songs as well—again, preferably in your key. (Accompaniments on other instruments besides piano are acceptable substitutes.) Again, follow along with the vocal score as you listen.

If you can't get a commercial recording of the accompaniment, the next best thing is for you to find a professional pianist to play it, while you record it. Or, if you are a good pianist, you can record yourself playing the piano part. You can then sing along with this recording. It may also work for you to sing the piece a cappella (unaccompanied), if you are good at sight singing.

Also play the top line or bass line of the introduction, interludes, and postludes. Some authorities, myself included, believe that a singer does not really know a song until he or she is familiar with all the sounds and characteristics of the accompaniment. Some would go so far as to say that each note—especially the introduction, interlude, postlude, and all the contrapuntal and harmonic devices—should be a significant part of your awareness in thorough preparation of a song. I don't think that this is necessary, and there are certainly great singers who do not have this level of knowledge of the music they sing. Some do, and that is fine, too.

Go over the words and music together, to get a general feeling for the song and become familiar with its style. Read the words with moderate loudness and at a moderate tempo. Work at deepening your understanding of the text and what it expresses. Write the words down from memory several times, while you hear yourself singing the song in your mind's ear or while you are actually singing.

In your mind, hear the song sung as it is written. If you feel the written tempo is too fast for you, do it at a comfortable tempo first. When you feel more at ease, you can do it as written. If you are trying to learn a song you've heard done by a pop singer, bear in mind that these artists very often don't sing the songs exactly as written. They change the pitch and duration of notes, dynamics, rhythm, tempo, and accompaniment. Folk singers may also sing another version of the song you have. In such cases, the score you have may not match the recording you like. Listen more to the artist's version of the accompaniment, once you know the words and melody, and practice singing along with it. Whatever version you choose, remember that when you perform it you will have to supply your accompanist or band with a written score showing the same version you are singing.

If you can write music, transcribe the melody from memory a number of times. It also helps if you write down distinctive musical features from the introduction, interlude, and postlude. If you are good at visualizing, you can visualize the words and melody in front of you, as well as the top and bottom lines of the introduction, the interludes and postludes, and other distinctive features in the score, including chords.

Pay attention to the places in the song where you inhale, so you can remember them. Also notice and keep in mind the moods and feelings of the song.

If you feel the song is too long for you to memorize straight through, you can divide it into parts and memorize section by section, finally putting the whole song together.

In the process of memorizing, don't actually sing the song too much; your voice will become tired. If you hear the song in your mind's ear, it will help you memorize more easily. If you are a beginner, the imagined song may sound a little vague to you, because your tonal image is not clearly formed. But with time and practice you will be able to know and hear what you want. Recordings and live performances of great artists will help you form a good tonal image too.

CONCLUSION

If you can memorize in the way just described, it will be to your advantage. If you can't, don't worry about it, because many famous singers don't know about harmony or counterpoint. Moreover, many singers all over the world sing without the ability to read music. For instance, in the oral tradition of folk music, people have learned to sing and play songs without reading music, just by listening and singing along. It will be much better, however, if you do learn to read music. It is always more desirable to have a thorough knowledge of whatever you are doing.

Some people feel that a detailed analytical approach helps them to memorize. If you are not one of them, or are not good at analyzing, don't be concerned.[4] Try the centuries-old Taoist approach, which trusts more in your intuitive power. You should still approach your memorizing with discipline and regularity, but don't struggle to learn your songs. Open your being and let your feelings and thoughts respond spontaneously to the words and music. Let the words and music flow into you. This will help to dissolve any blocks you may have with memorizing.

Once you have memorized a song, you will notice the rewards of your efforts. You will be able to sing with proper diction, tempo, rhythm, dynamics, style, phrasing, and breathing. With your attention free to focus entirely on singing, you will be able to interpret your song with feeling and a clear understanding of the lyrics and music. I encourage you to sing your song often and with complete enjoyment, performing it regularly for an audience. This will help you to become a better singer and interpreter and to retain the song in your memory.

Singing with a Variety of Tonal Color

In the words of my teacher, Alexander Kipnis, acclaimed as one of the great basses of the world, "Singing with a variety of tonal color is a very important element in expressive and artistic singing. Without it, no matter how properly the singer's voice is produced, his singing will soon become uninteresting." I am sure many authorities and professionals share this viewpoint.

Mr. Kipnis knew of what he spoke. He himself sang with a great variety of tonal color. Besides that warm, dark, and deep color a male low voice is meant to have, he excelled in producing a bright, brilliant white and many other colors as well. If you are fortunate enough to hear some of the currently available recordings by Kipnis, you will notice that his voice is not only beautiful and powerful, but is also colored by interesting tonal variation. His singing is expressive and artistic. He believed that the variation of tonal color was primarily created by the singer's feeling and sensitivity. The mere "technique" of coloring the voice could help only to a certain extent.

The methods I use to teach tonal color are largely drawn from my work with Kipnis. In this section we will discuss the more general "warm," "bright," and "dark" tonal colors, as well as other more specific ones.

PRODUCING A WARM COLOR

When you begin to learn to sing you should develop your tone to have a warm color, as it is primary and essential. You find this color by imagining and feeling that your tone is warm. You may imagine and feel the warmth of sunshine or the glowing quality of a friend. Also imagine and feel that your tone is round, whether you sing the vowel "ah" or the vowel "ee." Let your mouth opening be as round and free of tension as possible. The vowel "ee" requires a small, somewhat flattened oval mouth opening.

Your voice should be produced without strain and should have a round, concentrated tone with depth as well as good resonance.

With this warm tone as your fundamental color, you can go on to other colors without much difficulty. Some people have the warm color by nature, but sometimes they may lose it temporarily. It is always good to have a reliable image or feeling by which to conjure warmth, for use in time of need.

PRODUCING A BRIGHT COLOR

In general, a bright tonal color expresses delight and happiness. For instance, when you are happy and feel as though you want to laugh or smile, your voice usually will show a bright tonal color. When you are singing a happy song, try to sense its happy feeling. If you smile a little, your voice will brighten and help you express happiness. Whenever you smile or laugh when singing, maintain an open throat and remain flexible and relaxed so that your voice does not sound shrill or thin.

PRODUCING A DARK COLOR

A dark tonal color usually expresses sorrow or frustration. For instance, if your loved one has left you or you have just lost a good job and you feel sad, your voice will have a dark or somber color to it. To produce such a color, as with the others, you use your imagination to sense the unhappy feeling of the song. Also imagine that your voice is dark and deep. Shade your "ah" vowel with a little bit of an "aw" or "oh" sound, and open your mouth just a little bit more while maintaining an open feeling in the upper throat. Sing the vowels "ee" and "ay" with an almost round mouth opening. I sometimes imagine, while singing the vowel "ah" with an open throat, that the shape in my upper throat is oval. This also helps to darken the voice.

Be sure that your voice is free of strain, does not sound dull, and retains good resonance. Don't push your chin down against your neck. Some singers try to darken their voices this way and end up hurting their vocal cords.

Finally, it is very important that you keep your energy up while singing a sad song. Even though you are conjuring the feeling of unhappiness, you must not lose your vitality.

PRODUCING OTHER SPECIFIC COLORS

There are times when you have to use your imagination to create a specific tonal color. For instance, in Franz Schubert's great song, "The Wanderer," the last line, which reads, "Where you are not, there is happiness," is said by a ghostly voice. Regarding his thoughts on this line, Mr. Kipnis said, "That ghostly voice is very cold in my imagination, without warmth or sympathetic feeling." He demonstrated what he meant by this very effectively. As he sang this text, his imagination turned his voice into something cold, without any vibrato and with no obvious dynamic change. While he was singing the German word *ist* (which means "is" in English) in his low range, he stretched his lips sideways into a grimace, and his eyes were open quite wide with an icy, harsh look.

"The Erl-King" is another great song by Schubert, and Mr. Kipnis' interpretation of it is considered to have been supreme.[5] There are four characters—the narrator, the father, the young son, and the Erl-King. All are sung by the same person, and each voice has its own character and varied tonal colors, responding to the text and the music. The following are my notes on what Mr. Kipnis told me about how he developed the vocal colors for this piece:

> First I imagined how each voice should sound; then I created a specific fundamental tonal color to fit each voice. As I was singing and the drama of the song unfolded, my emotions, feelings, and tonal colors changed in response to the text and the music. If someone asked me how I colored my voice for each of the four characters, I would say that my imagination, emotional response to each character, and intuition always played a major part.

There is a wide spectrum of tonal color between very dark and very bright. The ability to use these colors consciously or unconsciously for appropriate emotional expression depends on the singer's natural endowment, sensitivity, training, and practice. Two great singers may not use the same tonal color to interpret the same song or the same musical phrase. Not only does each singer's voice have its own characteristics, making it as individual as a fingerprint, but so is each singer's emotional response unique. Therefore we cannot expect anyone, not even a great teacher, to impart to us all of the secrets of the spectrum of tonal color. A teacher can only show us, to a certain extent, the technique used in coloring the voice. To achieve what we want, we must each find our own way—our Tao—by which we bring our experience and feelings to bear in the application of the teacher's way or technique.

The goal can be expressed as, "I become what I sing," or, as Walt Whitman wrote, "I become what I behold." The singer, the singing, and the song become one.

Developing and Using Your Vocal Identity

Obviously each one of us has a voice that is different, with an inborn character of its own. Why then should we be concerned about vocal identity? Developing and using the identity *already in your voice* is to reveal its distinctive features and potential, allowing you to express freely, directly, and effectively your feelings, thoughts, and spirit. This does not happen automatically. It is true that your voice already has its identity, but you must help it to blossom.

Vocal identity is not a straitjacket, however; it is enhanced by versatility and flexibility. These allow you to keep your identity while changing style from one situation to another. Given the proper talent and training, you can go from opera to pop and from Shakespeare to American musical theater without loosing your identity.

Whether you study formally or informally or are self-taught, your training should give you a firm foundation and strong technique for developing your voice. Then you can select its good qualities and polish them for your use, at the same time eliminating its weaknesses. Sometimes you can even capitalize on weak or funny traits as comedians do. An actress like Marilyn Monroe, for instance, made very good use of her high, thin voice, proving that defects sometimes can be turned into virtues.

We all recognize identity in the speaking/acting voice. To a degree, identity in the singing voice is an extension of this. An obvious example would be my teacher, Alexander Kipnis, whose speaking voice sang. His vocal identity was in its timbre—the tonal quality and texture. Another example is Rex Harrison, whose singing voice sounded very much like his speaking voice, when he performed in "My Fair Lady" in the musical theater. But these are unusual cases; more often a singer has to discover the logical carry-over qualities. This is done through training with teachers, critical self-analysis during practicing and performing, and by listening to others' voices.

It is important to notice the special qualities of each voice. Richness and a ringing quality were the hallmarks of the voice of the great tenor Jussi Bjoerling. Maria Callas did not have the most beautiful voice, but she did have two virtues that gave her identity. First, and most important, her meticulous phrasing (musicianship) was unique. Second, her voice had a haunting timbre, which some people heard as a touch of oboe. She realized this strength and built her identity upon it.

Great singers in the same field can have completely different vocal identities or personalities. In Lieder, Dietrich Fischer-Dieskau and Hermann Prey are both great baritones. Some listeners prefer Fischer-Dieskau's interpretation and style; others consider Prey's voice richer and warmer.

As students, you will also have opinions about the singers you hear—good and bad. But you should take care not to attempt to imitate even your favorites, for this not only would be a dangerous strain on your voice, but also would defeat your aim of developing vocal identity. Everything you learn about the technique of singing will help you mold and change your sound, in the search for identity. The techniques that I write about in this book should be of great help to you.

The process is one of defining your strengths and weaknesses and of imagining what you want in your voice. On your part, this requires objectivity, which is not always easy to achieve. You may find yourself hearing the sound you hope to make, instead of the sound you actually are making. You can help develop your ability for objectivity and self-criticism by asking for feedback from others and by listening to recordings of yourself. As you develop both your ability to produce and control sound and your ability to be your own objective hearer, you can make choices about your vocal identity, choosing to build in the direction of the tonal qualities and textures that you most like and that are your strongest features.

With the help of experience, let your vocal identity bloom. Cultivate and treasure your own voice; it is the only one of its kind in the world.

Elements of Interpretation

After you have memorized a song and you can sing with little vocal difficulty, it is time to interpret the song. Ultimately the significance of all music resides in its emotional content and meaning.

At this stage a well-developed vocal technique, good diction, and an enthusiastic attitude will definitely help you use your voice to express fully what you feel and what you want to emphasize. Of equal important is sound musicianship, which includes singing on pitch, in rhythm, in time, with the required dynamics, and in style. Expressive acting ability is an added advantage.

A broad cultural background and constant observation of life will be very helpful, too. Stella Adler, a great American acting teacher, often urged her students to observe life around them so that they would be able to play various parts with better understanding and deeper insight into the characters.

How important is your own individuality in the part you sing or play? As Alexander Kipnis told me,

> Acting is to meld your own individuality with the character you sing or play, to make two into one. It would be wrong to say that an actor must forget his own individuality in order to transform himself completely into the character, because that would be impossible. You have your own voice, body, and feelings, and you cannot forget all these things. As you act, fifty percent of the character may legitimately be your own. The percentage can go even higher with some highly individualistic actors or singers.

Or, as the celebrated Russian actor, director, and teacher Konstantin Stanislavski advised, "Never lose yourself on the stage. Always act in your own person, as an artist. You can never get away from yourself."[6]

Regarding emotion and intellect, the legendary tenor Enrico Caruso said, "When I sing with the head alone I do not sing, I go through the opera like a machine. But with the heart also, I feel happy in my singing all over. I make everybody glad."[7]

Emphasizing the importance of intuition in the process of creativity, the great cellist Pablo Casals expressed this thought:

> Intuition is the decisive element in both the composing and the performance of music. Of course technique and intelligence have vital functions—one must master the technique of an instrument in order to extract its full potentialities, and one must apply one's intelligence in exploring every facet of the music—but ultimately, the paramount role is that of intuition. For me, the determining factor in creativity, in bringing a work to life, is that of musical instinct.[8]

Casals was 96 years of age when he made this observation, spoken very much like a Taoist.

When you first perform a song, you may not feel as free and spontaneous in your interpretation as these masters, and you may even make some mistakes. But don't worry; this is natural, and the more you perform the better you will become and the more likely it is that you will "become" the song.

Interpretation of song can be expressed in terms of the Taoist principle of interflow of elements in circular movement. As shown in Figure 39, interpreting a song involves the harmonious interflow of intuition, understanding, memorization, vocal technique, musicianship, and expressivity. In interpreting a song, you simply let it bloom like a flower!

FIGURE 39

Transforming Stage Fright into Stage Joy: An East-West Approach

Stage fright means fear and nervousness felt when appearing before an audience. It results from fear of uncertainty, fear that something disastrous may happen to your performance (your voice may sound terrible, you may crack on those climactic high notes, or your memory may slip, causing you to forget words and music). You may even worry about how you look. Behind all of these fears lurks the fear of loss of love, loss of respect, and loss of livelihood. So stage fright can cause much tension and nervousness. It can really prevent you from doing your best, or it can even cause you to do your worst.

As Ralph Waldo Emerson observed, however, "Knowledge is the antidote to fear." To know your problems and to know what you can do best and how to achieve it will definitely help you reduce fear. But without constantly practicing what you know, you will achieve little in eliminating your stage fright. As an old Chinese proverb says, "The purpose of learning is to put into use what you have learned."

The following guidelines will help you eliminate stage fright. Practice them constantly so you will not only dissolve stage fright, but turn it into stage joy!

• Cultivate an enthusiastic attitude of sharing your joy of singing with the audience.

• If you take pleasure in singing, you will not invite nervousness and tension, and instead you will create a harmonious feeling within yourself, which will free you from tension. So, enjoy the feeling of singing, and concentrate on the voice, the music, the words, the feeling, and the movement. Concentrate on what you plan to do onstage. After awhile, the act of concentration becomes a natural part of you; you will be able to concentrate without concentrating! This is one of the essences of Taoism.

• Avoid trying to prove how great you are, or you will be inviting nervousness and tension, placing yourself under an undue amount of pressure and responsibility for achieving greatness. A desire to prove how great you are implies a feeling of personal uncertainty, which in turn brings fear.

• Don't sing a song you don't like, even though the song has been acclaimed by critics and sung by famous singers. In Taoist terms, singing songs you don't like is a way of not acting in tune with Nature, which will produce an inharmonious feeling within you.

• Sing the songs you feel you can deliver with ease, both technically and emotionally.

• Know your songs thoroughly, not just through memorization of words, music, phrasing, tempo, and dynamics, but also by understanding the underlying meaning of the words. You should feel and understand the emotions and moods of each song.

• Practice the song until you feel confident that you have learned it.

• Shortly before you go onstage, do the body movement exercises and Moving Meditation described in Chapter 3. Breathe moderately, slowly, smoothly, deeply, and without being rigid. This will stimulate energy flow and counteract tension. In addition, you can do the Courage exercise described at the end of this section.

- Participate in many activities that require you to face an audience, such as acting, choral singing, public speaking, and debate.
- Cultivate a love and enthusiasm for sharing your feelings and thoughts with the audience, through your performance. The more you perform with love and enthusiasm, the faster your stage fright will disappear.

Even after you have used these guidelines and exercises for some time, you may still feel nervous before a performance. Don't feel badly, because it is very natural and you are in good company! As Luciano Pavarotti, the great Italian tenor, once said in a television interview, "If somebody tells you that he is not nervous before a performance, he is a liar."

Once you are onstage, just concentrate on your voice, the words, the music, and whatever you are supposed to do at that time. Your nervous tension and stage fright will be reduced as you enjoy your singing more and more. You will be at ease with both yourself and others, and you will transform stage fright into stage joy.

Courage Exercise

The following is a body movement exercise that is particularly helpful in eliminating fear and tension.

1. Stand erect with your feet apart about shoulder width and your knees slightly bent. Let your arms hang relaxed at your sides.
2. Make loose fists with your hands, with the backs facing out. Bend your arms slightly.
3. Raise your fists to the front of your body, to about shoulder height.
4. Pull your elbows back along the sides of your body, although not touching it. Then move your elbows up and forward in a circular motion, so your arms and fists move like the shafts on the wheels of an old steam locomotive. At the same time, rotate your shoulders along with your arms and let your elbows bend and straighten automatically, as needed to produce the circular motion. Let your body move up and down with the up and down movements of the elbows.

5. Repeat steps 3 and 4, making about twenty circles, starting the movement slowly, then gradually accelerating.

Do two or three sets of these circles. For best results, do two or three sets several times a week. If you have heart trouble, consult your doctor first.

While you are doing this exercise, close your mouth and let the tip of your tongue comfortably touch your upper palate. According to Taoist practice, when you put your tongue in this position, you spiritually connect heaven and earth. Physically you produce saliva to help prevent your throat from getting dry. As you accelerate your rotation, you will inhale and exhale faster and faster.

Fear and tension make your muscles contract and your brain shut down. This body movement exercise will help relax you, and your entire body will warm up very quickly. As you do it, think to yourself, "This powerful circular movement is chasing away my fear and tension and generating my courage." Notice yourself gaining courage.

7

Guidelines for Effective Practicing

The wise student hears of the Tao and practices it diligently. The average student hears of the Tao and gives it thought now and then. The foolish student hears of the Tao and laughs aloud. If there were no laughter, the Tao would not be what it is. . . . The Tao alone nourishes and brings everything to fulfillment.

LAO TZU

In the learning process, the formation of new habits is usually hampered to some degree by old habits. However, if you practice the new habits with love, care, regularity, and patience and with a strong desire to transform yourself, your new habits will take over. This chapter contains guidelines for your use in training yourself to practice vocalizing and singing effectively.

Begin by having a definite idea of what you want to work on or improve during your practice session. For instance, you may want to improve the sound of your high notes or low notes, your vowel sound "ee" or "ah," or the transition from a very soft sound to a very loud sound and vice versa. Or, you may wish to try out certain thoughts, images, or feelings that will help you respond spontaneously to a song you are singing. Perhaps you want to learn two new songs, or to practice three numbers you will be performing in an upcoming concert, or to improve the phrasing of a particular song. Or, you may simply want to go over the vocal exercises described in Chapter 4, to warm up your voice and keep it in good shape.

Set an approximate time limit for your practice session. One or two hours or longer is a good length, but even half an hour will help. If you are short of time, you can work on the things needing your immediate attention. When you have extra time, work on other things in the order of their importance.

Begin work by doing the body movement exercises and Moving Meditation (see Chapter 3), which will help you focus your attention and stimulate your energy flow. Following this, do several minutes of open-throat exercises (see Chapter 5).

Vocalize first in your middle range, then let your best notes lead you to the other notes. Even highly trained singers have some notes, certain vowels, or vowels in combination with certain consonants that sound better than others. Use soft or moderate dynamics to start with; don't sing *fortissimo* or loud high notes before you are warmed up and have good resonance.

When you are having problems with certain notes in a song, especially high notes, or if you feel you don't like the songs you have decided to practice, first sing the songs that are easy for you, that inspire you, or that you like, and then work on the problems. If, after a few minutes, you still cannot sing a certain high note the way you want it to sound, leave it alone. Do the vocal exercises in this book that help free you to sing with good resonance, flexibility, and good tonal quality. Then go back to the high note for several minutes. Be creative. Don't bore yourself by repeating certain exercises. Try to remember other exercises or musical phrases that have helped you in the past to get to that high note.

Rather than working on one or two songs to the exclusion of others, choose a variety of pieces, including some you have never sung before.

Change the pattern of your movements, including your hand movements. If you usually practice your continuous circular movement with your right hand, or if you are used to standing with your body weight on your right foot, then use your left hand or foot or use both left and right alternately.[1] You will also feel more flexible if you gently move your weight back and forth over the balls of your feet. Always avoid standing on your heels and locking your knees.

During practice you can dance or move around in a variety of patterns while you are vocalizing or singing. This will accustom you to being relaxed and spontaneous, even though in an actual concert performance of classical music you are expected, for the most part, to move very little.

Look into the mirror occasionally to check your facial expression, mouth opening, posture, or movement.

Use a type of mental exercise called an *imagery rehearsal* to adopt good, positive attitudes about your singing. Imagery rehearsals are like programmed tapes for your brain. Greg Louganis, the 1984 Olympic gold medalist in diving, is just one of many athletes who have used imagery rehearsals successfully.

While waiting for his turn, he went over his next dive in his mind. These can be just as effective for singers. The following are two examples.

- Spend a few minutes or more imagining how you would like to sound while singing a song. Imagine you are singing all the notes with ease, whether they are lyrical, dramatic, high, low, very loud, or very soft.

- Imagine that you are in the audience, listening and watching yourself sing, with the purpose of directing your own performance. Then go one step further by imagining that you are walking toward yourself on stage and then merging with yourself. Get up and sing, not in your imagination, but with your real voice. Do this imagery rehearsal with a sense of fun, as if you were a child playing a game. You will be amazed at how your imagination can help you to improve your singing quickly, getting you closer to what you want.

Another mental exercise is derived from the words of Walt Whitman, quoted earlier: "I become what I behold." As a singer, this means that you become what you hear. It means the singer, the singing, and the song become one. The hearer, the hearing, and the heard become one. The song becomes you, and you become the song. This is one of the most exciting and rewarding moments you can have as an artist. If you keep this belief present in your mind, it will help to create such a moment. Sometimes it will happen when you are practicing. When it does, notice it, feel it, try to remember it. Dance in celebration for what you have achieved. Because people tend to remember things better at moments sparked with high spirits, you will most likely be able to re-create the wonderful moment again, whether in practice or in actual performance.

There are other ways that you can open yourself up, creating the potential for such a joyful moment. Sometimes I feel my channels opening up and joyful energy flowing through me while I am walking and looking at the beauty of Nature around me: blossoming flowers, sparkling streams, sunlit leaves, infinite bright blue sky, floating white clouds, mountains, valleys, a rainbow, raindrops like liquid sunshine, a peaceful starry night, and other enchanting things. Sometimes this state of being will come to me when I am inspired by expressive or exciting music, singing, dancing, or drama, or from the warmth and vibrant contact of someone I love. Whenever you feel this way, make a special point of noticing both the feeling and whatever it was that awakened it in you. You can use your memory of these moments of ecstasy to heighten your energy when engaged in the more everyday activities of practice.

Sometimes you may need to hear a song interpreted by great artists in order to find the vibration (whether sonic, musical, or spiritual), the tonal image, and the expression you are searching for. Besides going to their live performances, you can listen to their recordings; you can dance or move to their singing or simply sit, listen, and absorb.

Play the recording at a moderate volume; if it is too loud it will not sound real—the voice will be amplified bigger than the actual sound is. When you hear a big, amplified sound, you may be tempted to imitate it, unconsciously forcing your voice to sound big. It is also important to be aware that, like fingerprints, no two voices are alike; no two vocal organs are exactly the same in size, shape, and strength; and no two people's emotional responses are exactly the same in style or intensity. While listening to great artists singing, then, realize that your voice is different. Although their voices may serve as good examples, you will not be able to copy them.

When listening to the singing of great artists, feel it and absorb it; let it inspire you. You can even dance or do other movements to their singing, letting yourself express the feelings they evoke. You can then apply this energy to your own practicing.

If you have a good tape recorder, record your voice once in a while, play it back, and check what is good and what is not so good. Set a time limit; otherwise you can use a lot of time in recording. When possible, have a pianist rehearse with you, then record yourself singing with this accompaniment. Again, listen critically to your singing, and to how well you and the pianist are working together.

When you are sick or very tired, don't force yourself to practice.

Last but not least, cultivate a habit of enthusiasm and enjoyment in practicing. You do this by keeping an open and smiling heart, a burning interest in practicing regularly, an association with people who are supportive of your work, and an understanding of the necessity for patience. Otherwise, you will be creating mental or emotional blocks that will in turn affect your voice production and singing. Without the feeling of enthusiasm and enjoyment, your practice will not accomplish the good results it should, and your performance will not show you at your best. Recall this statement from the *I Ching*: "The secret of all natural and human law is movement that meets with devotion. . . . Because enthusiasm shows devotion to movement, heaven and earth are at its side and move with it."

8

An East-West Approach to Maintaining Good Health

Sound mind, sound body, sound voice.

THE AUTHOR

Good mental and physical health are vital to everyone, especially to those of you who are pursuing the career of a professional singer, actor, or speaker. Since the instrument you play—your voice—is in your throat, and since it is the most sensitive musical instrument there is, any weakening of your physical strength, any discomfort in the throat, and any emotional disturbance will adversely affect your tonal quality and your appearance. Remember, the mind and body are closely related and interdependent; the health of the one affects the health of the other. So, it is essential for you to keep healthy in every way.

The following are suggestions for helping you to maintain good mental and physical health.

Mental Health

- Enjoy loving and being loved.
- Be peaceful with yourself and others.
- Be compassionate toward yourself and others. (This is a particularly strong aspect of Buddhist philosophy.)

- Have few desires. (This is a strength of Taoist philosophy.) As Socrates said, "Those who want the fewest things are dearest to the Gods."

- Follow the Taoist direction of appreciating the feeling of contentment.

- Remember the Chinese proverb, "You are as rich as the radius of your imagination." Let your imagination glow, grow, and fly.

- Recognize and experience suffering as an inherent part of the process of personal growth. Buddhism teaches that suffering will open channels for you to look into yourself as well as understand and sympathize with others on a much deeper level.

- Appreciate the good qualities in yourself and in others.

- Recognize your own weaknesses, and take corrective action.

- Although worrying is only human, the less you do it, the better, because it can destroy your health. Rather than worrying, discern which problems you can fix and which you cannot. The fourteenth Dalai Lama, spiritual leader of Tibet, has said that there is no use worrying about situations that cannot be fixed. It is important, instead, to apply your energy and time to problems that can be solved. Your ability to remedy the situation will also help develop self-confidence. Remember this popular Western prayer: "God grant me the serenity to accept the things we cannot change, the courage to change the things I can, and the wisdom to know the difference."

- If you have failed to accomplish what you want to do, think of your life as a long journey toward a destination, and that the failure is only a temporary stopover. Another failure is simply another temporary stopover. You must continue your journey with faith.

- As Pablo Casals said at the age of 96, "Feel as if you are reborn each day and rediscover the world of nature of which you joyfully are a part."[1]

- Keep a "smiling heart." In following this Taoist philosophy you will feel your heart and your whole being opening up, unblocking the channels for the flow of your vital energy (ch'i).

- Laugh as often as you can. Laugh at your own folly as well.

- Cry if you feel you need to. Cry for sorrow, cry for happiness, cry for any other reason.

- Meditate regularly.

- Have at least one good hobby, such as painting, photography, gardening, growing plants, or playing a musical instrument.

Physical Health

To maintain good physical health, it is important to exercise regularly. Movement can be vigorous but should not be strenuous. Avoid exercises that will tighten your throat, such as certain forms of weight lifting. Do the body movement exercises and Moving Meditation in Chapter 3, as well as other exercises that appeal to you and suit you. These can include swimming, yoga, T'ai Chi Ch'uan, Qigong, and a variety of physical fitness exercises and dance movements. Brisk walking and jogging, although they have limited variations of movement, are beneficial to a certain extent.

Maintain proper posture in sleeping, standing, sitting, and walking. Good posture will help your breathing and blood circulation as well as help you relax and conserve energy. A centuries-old Chinese principle for maintaining good posture, which has universal meaning, is as follows:[2]

> Sleep like a bow
> Stand like a pine
> Sit like a bell
> Walk like the wind

This advice is interpreted as follows:

- A bow is curved. When you sleep on your side, with your body slightly curved, not straight, you'll feel most relaxed.

- A pine is strong, sturdy, and erect, but it also shows flexibility when blown by wind. When you stand like a pine, you have strength and a certain degree of flexibility.

- The old Chinese bell was long, straight, and firm, unlike the curved Western bell. To sit like a bell means your spine is straight and steady, allowing the natural forces in the body to vibrate.

- The wind moves without weight. To walk like the wind means your body is light and flowing and you are conserving your energy. (You can jog like the wind, too.)

It is important that you sleep adequately. Take a nap or rest in between long hours of working or running around. If you must sit for long periods, move around for awhile every two hours or so.

Eat a well-balanced diet, including salads and plenty of other fresh fruits and vegetables. Learn to cook your food until it is just done but not overcooked. Avoid eating processed food, as well as skipping meals or overeating. Eating too much keeps you from breathing deeply and inhibits flexible movement. The Taoist also views overeating as an obstruction to meditation, because it blocks the inner psychic centers and the mind.[3]

Avoid smoking and drugs. Before singing, avoid intoxicating or iced drinks and spicy foods. Stay away from mucus-producing foods or drinks such as milk, yogurt, beer, and buttermilk. If you must, try them and see whether they affect your voice adversely. Wait two hours after a full meal before singing.

Get plenty of fresh air, and try not to spend long hours in poorly ventilated places.

Dress sensibly. In cold weather, don't run around with your neck and chest exposed, or go out right after taking a bath or washing your hair. Keep your feet warm.

Don't talk while you are in a draft; in any case, get away from a draft as soon as you can. Talk in moderation, especially before a performance, or you will tire your voice. Some singers avoid talking altogether before a performance.

Don't overindulge in sex; it saps your energy.

Treat infected teeth and gums quickly. Have chronically infected tonsils and adenoids removed, as the infection will affect your throat. Avoid close contact with people who have severe colds, throat ailments, or contagious diseases.

Rest a day or so if you begin to have a sore throat, a cold, or laryngitis, which are common ailments and frustrations to singers, actors, and public speakers. If you take a day off, you will have a very good chance of recovering quickly. On the other hand, if you continue to use your voice a lot and run around when you have laryngitis or a sore throat, your condition will most likely get worse, and it will take longer to recover. It is advisable to see a doctor if the condition persists, because a serious throat ailment or cold may also affect your hearing, and it can spread infection to other parts of your body.

Massage the bottoms of your feet for a few minutes before going to bed and before getting up, or whenever you feel you need it. This can help stimulate blood circulation and relax nervous tension. Use the following centuries-old Taoist method of foot massage:[4]

- With your right palm, rub the bottom of your left foot in a continuous circular movement. You may want to put your left palm on the back of your right hand to help the rubbing. Then reverse and massage your right foot.

- Use your feet to rub each other, as an alternative to using your hands, with the sole of one foot rubbing against the instep of the other.
- Use the middle of the ball of one foot (which the Chinese call the "bubbling spring") to rub the other, and vice versa. This is especially good for the kidneys.
- Use the arch of one foot to massage the side and ankle of the other, and vice versa.
- Massage your toes with your thumb and forefinger.

Take good care of your feet, not only because they support your weight and help you move around, but also because their ailments may affect your digestion, blood circulation, nervous system, heart, and brain—indeed, your whole body.

For good health of the inner organs, the Taoists recommend practicing the following six therapeutic sounds for several minutes every day. Practice each sound six times as one set.

"Ha"	for the heart
"Hu"	for the spleen
"Sssss"	for the lungs
"Shi"	for the solar plexus
"Shü"	for the liver
"Fu"	for the kidneys

Note that "ü" (in "shü") is pronounced by holding your lips as if you are pronouncing "oo" (as in "too"), but then actually saying "ee" (as in "see"). The vowel at the end of each sound should hardly be pronounced at all. Rather, it indicates the shape of the mouth as you blow out air after the consonant (much like blowing out a candle). Keep all the sounds short and within your comfortable speaking range. Practice with enthusiasm, but don't "push" the sound out.

To maintain the good health of your vocal instrument, it is very important that you not strain your voice by incorrect voice production. Avoid singing or talking too loudly or at high pitch, or by opening your mouth too much and/ or forcing out a great deal of breath. Frequent straining of your throat will be harmful to your voice. Nodes may be formed on your vocal cords and will affect the good quality of your voice. Removal of the nodes by surgery does not guarantee that your voice will recover fully. On the other hand, if you sing or talk without straining your voice, the deep breathing and good sonic vibrations will definitely be beneficial to your physical health.

Conclusion: Singing and the Body-Mind-Spirit Connection

There are many stories that could be told of the healing and health-sustaining powers of music. Most likely you could tell a few yourself. I will mention here, in concluding this chapter, two sources of support for singing as therapy, from the mental health field.

The first comes from Paul Nordoff and Clive Robbins, who, in their book *Music Therapy in Special Education*, talk of their use of singing to help their students release hidden emotions. They find that it is a powerful tool in helping children with handicaps and mental retardation, as well as being a delight for normal people. Singing comes naturally to children, so all they need is encouragement to participate and an enthusiastic response.[5]

The second comes from Dr. John M. Bellis, a psychiatrist whose work was reviewed in a 1979 issue of *Prevention* magazine. He makes extensive use of bioenergetic therapy in his practice. This is a process pioneered by Dr. Alexander Lowen, and it posits a crucial connection between a person's state of body and state of mind. Repressions of anxiety are believed to be reflected in the body's musculature. According to bioenergetic theory, repressions of anxiety, and eventually the anxiety itself, are relieved through the release of muscular and emotional tension. Dr. Bellis finds that people discover in music and song the possibility of giving expression to thoughts and feelings they could not otherwise articulate. With the body as instrument, Dr. Bellis sees the use of the voice and singing as a way that we integrate experience internally, resulting in the release of tension.[6]

When you sing well, especially with a properly produced and expressive voice, you will create powerful sonic and emotional vibrations that can move you, elevate your spirit, stretch your mind, and sometimes even make you feel that you are suddenly taking flight, soaring, and extending far beyond yourself. Such vibrations, by releasing nervous tension, will generate energy for you as well as soothe and bring peace to your mind.

NOTES

Chapter 1

1. This book is also known as *The Book of Tao* and *The Tao Teh Ching*. Its greatness inspired the renowned author Lin Yutang to say, "If there is one book in the whole of Oriental literature which one should read above all the others, it is, in my opinion, Laotse's *Book of Tao*." Lin Yutang (Ed.), *The Wisdom of China and India* (New York: Random House, 1942), p. 579. (Author's note: Laotse is a variation on the spelling of the name Lao-tzu and Lao Tzu.)

2. Fritjof Capra, *Tao of Physics* (New York: Bantam Books, 1984), pp. 101-102.

3. Ibid., p. 104. Capra quotes G. S. Kirk, *Heraclitus—The Cosmo Fragments* (Cambridge, England: University Press, 1970).

4. Chang Chung-yuan. *Creativity and Taoism* (New York: Harper & Row, 1970), p.5.

5. Richard Wilhelm and C. G. Jung, *The Secret of the Golden Flower: A Chinese Book of Life* (New York: Harcourt Brace Jovanovich, 1962), p. 86.

6. Edmond Bordeaux Szekely, *Creative Exercises for Health and Beauty* (Rutland, VT: Academy Book Publishers, 1976). Szekely uses da Vinci's drawings and notes in the Sforza Archives in Milan and Florence to reconstruct the artist's ideas about circular movement.

7. This is also known as "cavity of origin" and is considered by the Taoists to be one of the essential centers for meditation. In the Asian Indian tradition, the spot between and behind the eyebrows is called the "third eye." In the West, we also know this is the area of the brain where the pineal gland is located. Just below it is another important meditation center, called the "four-petaled lotus." Its function is to translate thoughts into action. I have found that, if I channel my desire for a

free and good tone or for expressive and beautiful singing through the third eye and through its neighboring four-petaled lotus, I can often create the sound I want.

Chapter 2

1. According to Dr. Jean Houston, this is an effective way to awaken your nondominant side, helping you to activate and coordinate more areas of your brain. She believes that, by making a practice of using both hands or both sides of your body often, you will increase your available brain power. When I asked her whether doing this while practicing vocal exercises would improve coordination for singing, she said "yes." This hypothesis has been supported by Dr. Houston's recent research. See Jean Houston, "The Left-Handed Way" in *Dromenon* (Pomona, New York: October, 1978), pp. 12-13.

Chapter 4

1. A diphthong is a "double vowel" sound that is spoken or sung as a single syllable. In forming a diphthong, you begin at or near the articulatory position for one vowel and glide to or toward the position for another. For example, the diphthong in "night" begins with a long "ah" sound and glides toward an "ee" sound before the final consonant is added.

Chapter 5

1. Some singers feel that the sinus cavities and postnasal cavities also give some resonance to the voice. Some voice authorities have conducted tests and have concluded that the resonance felt by singers in these areas, as well as in the chest area, does not affect the accoustical quality of the voice; that is, it adds nothing to the tone that reaches the ears of the audience. William Vennard, *Singing: The Mechanism and the Technic* (New York: Carl Fischer, 1967); M. A. Bunch, *Dynamics of the Singing Voice* (Vienna: Springer Verlag, 1982). Brodnitz has pointed out that the role of sinuses as resonating chambers is extremely doubtful. See Friedrich S. Brodnitz, *Keep Your Voice Healthy* (Boston: Little, Brown & Co., 1988), pp. 10-11.

Chapter 6

1. Carlo Lamperti, *Improving Your Voice* (New York: Vantage Press, 1954).
2. For further information on this subject, see Arthur Young, *Reflexive Universe* (New York: Delacorte Press, 1976); and J. White & S. Kuppiner (Eds.), *Future Science* (New York: Anchor/Doubleday, 1976).

3. Donal Henahan, "When Neurologists Study Song," *New York Times*, January 14, 1979, p. D19. Henahan is quoting here from pp. 145 and 152 of A. R. Damasio & H. Damasio, "Musical Faculty," in M. Critchley & R. A. Henson (Eds.), *Music and the Brain* (London: Heinemann Medical Books, 1977), pp. 141-155.

4. Ibid. Henahan notes that Hanna and Antonio Damasio have found that language and music unite in the right hemisphere, rather than shifting after training to the left, which is the more analytical hemisphere. "This could be why musical perception and expression, which relate so closely to emotional expression, hallmarks of right hemisphere function, remain somewhat distant from the analytical processes conducting reason from the left hemisphere" (p. D19).

5. We are fortunate that Kipnis's magnificent and deeply moving performance of this great song can now be heard in the recording entitled, "The Art of Alexander Kipnis" (Seraphim, LP 60076). I strongly suggest that you listen to this interpretation, as well as to his other recordings. We lost a great artist and teacher when he passed away at the age of eighty-seven in May 1978.

6. Konstantin Stanislavski, *An Actor Prepares* (Elizabeth R. Hapgood, Trans.) (New York: Theatre Arts Books, 1948), p. 167.

7. Frank E. Miller, *Vocal Art Science* (New York: G. Schirmer, 1927), p. 138.

8. American Photographic Book Publishing Company, *Casals, Photographed by Fritz Henle* (Garden City, NY: Author, 1975).

Chapter 7

1. See note 1 in Chapter 2.

Chapter 8

1. American Photographic Book Company, *op. cit.*

2. Da Liu, *The Tao of Health and Longevity* (New York: Schocken Books, 1978), p. 133. Reprinted by permission of Paragon House Publishers.

3. Lu K'uan Yu, *The Secrets of Chinese Meditation* (New York: Samuel Weiser, 1975), p. 124.

4. Da Liu, *op. cit.*, pp. 149-150. The Chinese have discovered that, from the leg down to the foot, there are three yin meridians, which affect the spleen, kidney, and liver; and three yang meridians, which affect the stomach, bladder, and gall bladder. When Master Liu demonstrated this foot massage and the proper postures described earlier, he noted, "Though these are simple things to do, they can certainly help you maintain good health."

5. Paul Nordoff & Clive Robbins, *Music Therapy in Special Education* (John Day Co., New York, New York, 1971).

6. Information on Lowen's and Bellis' work is taken from John Yates, "Make a Joyful Noise," *Prevention*, January 1979, pp. 50-51.

Bibliography

The following is a list of books on Taoism and related matters. They are all in English except as indicated.

Blofeld, John, *Taoism: The Road to Immortality* (Boulder, CO: Shambhala, 1978).

Blofeld, John, *Gateway to Wisdom* (Boulder, CO: Shambhala, 1980).

Bolen, Jean Shimoda, *The Tao of Psychology: Synchronicity and the Self* (New York: Harper & Row, 1979).

Capra, Fritjof, *The Tao of Physics* (New York: Bantam Books, 1984).

Chang, A. I., *The Tao of Architecture* (Princeton, NJ: Princeton University Press, 1981).

Chang, Chung-yuan, *Creativity and Taoism* (New York: Harper & Row, 1968).

Chang, Stephen T., *The Tao of Balanced Diet* (San Francisco: Tao Publishers, 1987).

Chang, Po-Tuan, *The Inner Teachings of Taoism* (Trans. by T. Cleary; commentary by Liu I-Ming) (Boston: Shambhala, 1986).

Ch'en, Lih-Fu (Ed.), *A Study of the Application of the Teaching of I Ching* (Taipeh, Taiwan: Chung Hwa Book Company, 1982). (In Chinese)

Cheng, Man-Jan, *Lao-Tzu: "My words are very easy to understand,"* Lectures on the Tao Teh Ching (Trans. by T. C. Gibbs) (Richmond, CA: North Atlantic Books, 1981).

Chia, Man-Tak, *Awaken Healing Energy Through the Tao* (New York: Aurora Press, 1983).

Chia, Man-Tak, *Taoist Way to Transform Stress into Vitality* (New York: Heal Tao Books, 1986).

Deng, Ming-Dao, *The Wandering Taoist* (San Francisco: Harper & Row, 1983).

Deng, Ming-Dao, *Seven Bamboo Tablets of the Cloudy Satchel* (San Francisco: Harper & Row, 1987).

Deng, Ming-Dao, *Gateway to a Vast World* (San Francisco: Harper & Row, 1989).

Dreher, Diane, *The Tao of Peace* (New York: Donald I. Fine, 1989).

Grigg, Ray, *The Tao of Relationships* (New York: Bantam Books, 1989).

Heider, John, *The Tao of Leadership* (New York: Bantam Books, 1986).

The I Ching or Book of Changes (Trans. by R. Wilhelm & C. Baynes) (Princeton, NJ: Princeton University Press, 1967).

Laotse, "The Book of Tao" ("The Tao Teh Ching") (Trans. by Lin Yutang), in Lin Yutang (Ed.), *The Wisdom of China and India* (New York: Random House, 1942), pp. 583-624.

Lao Tsu, "Tao Te Ching" (Trans. by Gia-Fu Feng & Jane English) (New York: Vintage Books, 1972.)

Liu, Da, *Taoist Health Exercise Book* (New York: Links Books, 1974).

Liu, Da, *The Tao of Health and Longevity* (New York: Schocken Books, 1978).

Liu, Da, *The Tao and Chinese Culture* (London: Routledge & Kegan Paul, 1981).

Lu, K'uan Yu (Charles Luk), *The Secrets of Chinese Meditation* (New York: Samuel Weiser, 1975).

Master Da-Tung, *The Philosophy of Lao Tzu* (Taipeh, Taiwan: Hwa Lien Publications, 1976). (In Chinese)

Messing, Robert, *The Tao of Management* (Atlanta: Humanics, 1988).

Nan, Hwai-Chin, *A Discourse on Zen and Tao* (Taipeh, Taiwan: Lao Ku Culture Company, 1982). (In Chinese)

Needham, Joseph (ed.), *Science and Civilization in China* (Vol. 3) (New York: Cambridge University Press, 1959).

Pasley, Sally, *The Tao of Cooking* (Berkeley, CA: Ten Speed Press, 1982).

Reid, Daniel P., *The Tao of Health, Sex, Longevity: A Modern Practical Guide to the Ancient Way* (New York: Simon and Schuster, 1989).

The Secret of the Golden Flower: A Chinese Book of Life (Trans. to German and explained by R. Wilhelm; commentary by C. G. Jung; trans. to English by C. F. Baynes) (New York: Harcourt, Brace & World, 1962).

Siu, Ralph G., *The Tao of Science* (Cambridge, MA: MIT Press, 1958).

Wieger, Leo, *Taoism* (Burbank, CA: Ohara Publications, 1976).

Wing, R. L., *The Tao of Power* (New York: Doubleday, 1986).

Index

For information about Professor Stephen Chun-Tao Cheng's
workshops and trainings, audio and video tapes, please write to:

Tao of Voice Center
395 Riverside Drive, Box 7A
New York, NY 10025